CHRISTOPHER ISHERWOOD

MODERN LITERATURE MONOGRAPHS
GENERAL EDITOR: Philip Winsor

In the same series:

(continued on last page of book)

CHRISTOPHER ISHERWOOD

Claude J. Summers

FREDERICK UNGAR PUBLISHING CO.
NEW YORK

For Ted-Larry Pebworth

the two of them absorbed in their books
yet so completely aware of each other's presence

Copyright © 1980 by Frederick Ungar Publishing Co., Inc.
Printed in the United States of America
Design by Anita Duncan

Library of Congress Cataloging in Publication Data

Summers, Claude J
  Christopher Isherwood.

  Bibliography: p.
  Includes index.
  1. Isherwood, Christopher, 1904–
—Criticism and interpretation.
PR6017.S5Z85   823'.912   80-5335
ISBN 0-8044-2846-8

148887

PR
6017
.S5
Z85
1980

Contents

Chronology

1933–34   In London, he works on the screenplay of *Little Friend*, a film directed by Berthold Viertel.

1934–37   Lives with Heinz in various European cities, seeking a haven where Heinz can avoid conscription into the German army.

1935   His third novel, *The Last of Mr. Norris*, is published.

1936   *The Dog Beneath the Skin*, a play written in collaboration with Auden, is produced in London.

1937   *The Ascent of F 6*, a second play written with Auden, is produced in London.

1938   *Lions and Shadows*, an autobiography, is published; the third of the Auden-Isherwood plays, *On the Frontier*, is produced in Cambridge; he and Auden travel to China.

January 1939   He and Auden emigrate to the United States.

1939   His fourth novel, *Goodbye to Berlin*, and a travel book written with Auden, *Journey to a War*, are published. He declares his pacificism. With an American lover, Vernon, he travels to California, where he settles and establishes friendships with Gerald Heard and Aldous Huxley. He converts to Vedantism and becomes a disciple of Swami Prabhavananda.

1940   He, Auden, Huxley, and Heard are attacked in the British press for abandoning England. At the death of an uncle, he inherits the Bradshaw-Isherwood estates, but renounces his rights in favor of his younger brother Richard. He begins scriptwriting for the Hollywood motion picture industry, an employment he pursues intermittently thereafter.

1941–42   Works at an American Friends Service Committee hostel for war refugees in Haverford, Pennsylvania.

1943–45   Edits *Vedanta and the West*, a periodical published by the Vedanta Society of Southern California.

1944   His translation of the Bhagavad Gita, prepared
           in collaboration with Swami Prabhavananda, is
           published.

1945   *Prater Violet*, his fifth novel, is published.

1946   Becomes a naturalized citizen of the United
           States.

1947   Publishes his and Swami Prabhavananda's col-
           laborative translation of *Shankara's Crest-
           Jewel of Discrimination* and his revised trans-
           lation of Baudelaire's *Journaux Intimes*.

1947–48   With his friend, the photographer William
           Caskey, he travels in South America.

1949   *The Condor and the Cows*, a travel book based
           on his South American trip, is published. He is
           elected to membership in the National Insti-
           tute of Arts and Letters.

1953   Publishes a translation, prepared with Swami
           Prabhavananda, of *How to Know God: The
           Yoga Aphorisms of Patanjali*. Begins a rela-
           tionship with Don Bachardy.

1954   His sixth novel, *The World in the Evening*, is
           published.

1959   Accepts an appointment as Visiting Professor
           at California State College, Los Angeles. He
           subsequently holds visiting professorships at
           the University of California, Santa Barbara; the
           University of California, Los Angeles; and the
           University of California, Riverside.

1962   His seventh novel, *Down There on a Visit*, is
           published.

1963   Presents a lecture series, "The Autobiography
           of My Books," at the University of Califor-
           nia, Berkeley. Publishes *An Approach to
           Vedanta*.

1964   *A Single Man*, his eighth novel, is published.

1965   Publishes a biography, *Ramakrishna and His
           Disciples*.

1966   *Exhumations*, a collection of stories, essays,
           and poems, is published.

1

That Enormous Journey: A Biographical Sketch

The art of Christopher Isherwood illustrates the definition of literature as a force of memory dimly understood. Few writers have so exclusively distilled their art from personal experience and so self-consciously blurred the boundaries separating autobiography and fiction. Since his life is the fundamental source of his work, an understanding of his literary career necessitates a knowledge of his biography.

He was born Christopher William Bradshaw-Isherwood on August 26, 1904.[1] An old and distinguished family, the Bradshaw-Isherwoods were among the principal landowners in Cheshire, England; their holdings included Marple Hall, a sprawling Elizabethan manor, and Wyberslegh Hall, a less pretentious country house where Christopher was born. Isherwood's father, Frank, was the second son of John Bradshaw-Isherwood, the head of the family. As a second son, Frank was expected to earn his own living—the family estate being entailed to his older brother, Henry—and he became a professional soldier, serving in such places as South Africa, Ireland, and finally, France.

Isherwood's mother, Kathleen, was the only child of Frederick Machell-Smith, a successful Bury wine merchant, and his wife, Emily Greene, whose brother Sir Walter Greene was a wealthy brewer. Kathleen and Frank married in 1903 after a long courtship and despite the objections of her father. After the birth of Christopher, the couple employed a nurse, Annie Avis, who was most responsible for the early upbringing of Christopher and his younger brother, Richard, who was born in 1911.

In 1914, Christopher was sent to a preparatory school in Surrey, St. Edmund's, which was run by two of Frank's cousins. While he was at St. Edmund's, in May of 1915, his father was killed in action near Ypres, France. Although Christopher did not feel the loss of his father very deeply at the time, the event was to affect him greatly in later years. His mother's grief made him jealous of his father, and the death engendered in the son an irrational shame at not having fought in the First World War. During his last year at St. Edmund's, he met a boy two and a half years his junior, W. H. Auden.

In early 1919, Isherwood entered Repton, a prestigious public school dating from the reign of Mary Tudor. At Repton, he was initially only an average pupil, but he won prizes in English; and, under the hypnotic influence of a gifted history teacher, G. B. Smith, he eventually became one of the school's most brilliant scholars. He formed close friendships with Hector Wintle and Edward Upward, both of whom were to become novelists. With the coaching of Smith, Isherwood won an eighty-pound scholarship to read history at Corpus Christi College, Cambridge.

In 1923, Isherwood joined Upward at Cambridge, where the latter had matriculated the previous year. Both young men quickly became disillusioned with the university's history program and unsuccessfully requested transfers to the English curriculum. They also became disillusioned with Cambridge social life and, by extension, with the social life of England. The two collaborated on surrealistic fantasies that satirized the hypocrisy of English society, setting the stories in an imaginary location named Mortmere. Their literary heroes at this time included Baudelaire, Wilfred Owen, Katherine Mansfield, Emily Brontë, and T. S. Eliot; and Isherwood became active in the Film Club. Meanwhile, they neglected their academic obligations. Unprepared for his examinations in 1925, Isherwood deliberately answered the questions facetiously and was asked to withdraw from the university.

Leaving Cambridge behind him in 1925, Isherwood took a job in London as part-time secretary to a string quartet led by André Mangeot. Becoming almost a member of the Mangeot family, he grew more and more alienated from his own mother. Heavily influenced by the work of a new literary hero, E. M. Forster, he also began to write novels; and he frankly acknowledged his homosexuality to himself and to his mother.

In December of 1925, he renewed his friendship with Auden, whom he was surprised to discover had become a poet. Then an undergraduate at Oxford, Auden cast Isherwood in the role of senior literary advisor and later introduced him to Stephen Spender, another Oxford undergraduate. The three became the central members of the "Auden Gang," the angry young men who dominated English literary life in the 1930s.

In May 1928, Isherwood's first novel, *All the Conspirators*, was published. A scathing dissection of middle-class malaise, the book received some good notices but sold poorly. Making one last effort to achieve success in his mother's eyes, Isherwood entered medical school at King's College, London, where Hector Wintle was already enrolled. Medical school proved a disaster, at least in part because Isherwood devoted most of his time to writing the first draft of his ambitious second novel, *The Memorial*. By Christmas of 1928, he realized that he would not complete his medical studies. At the suggestion of Auden, who had recently returned from Germany, Isherwood departed on March 14, 1929, for a brief visit to Berlin.

Isherwood's visit to Berlin in 1929 proved to be a decisive event in his life. He determined to live there. In Berlin, he felt released from the social and sexual inhibitions that stifled his development in England. The city's political excitement and sexual freedom became the stuff of his art. Precariously supporting himself on an allowance from his Uncle Henry and by giving English lessons, Isherwood found lodgings in shabbily genteel and working-class areas of the city. He immersed himself in the bohemian world of male prostitutes and lived unpretentiously, almost anonymously. At the same time, he worked very hard at revising his second novel and at translating his experience of the Berlin demimonde into what would eventually become the unsurpassed portrait of pre-Hitler Germany, the Berlin stories.

In March of 1932, Isherwood fell in love with Heinz, a German working-class youth. Meanwhile, the German political situation grew ever more dangerous as the Nazis became increasingly powerful. After Hitler's appointment as chancellor in 1933, Isherwood and Heinz decided to leave Germany, a decision made urgent by Heinz's eligibility for conscription into the German military. For the next four years, the two restlessly wandered from one European country to another, searching for a place where they could settle together. The odyssey finally ended when Heinz had to return to Germany, where he was arrested, sentenced to prison for homosexual activities with Isherwood, and then to service in the German army.

During the 1930s, Isherwood rapidly gained a reputation as the most promising novelist of his generation. *The Memorial* was well received on its publication in 1932, and *The Last of Mr. Norris* was an even greater success on its appearance in 1935. In addition, the publication of sections of *Goodbye to Berlin*, especially the "Sally Bowles" episode, which was issued separately as a novella in 1937, established him as a penetrating observer of the disturbing events in Germany. He became friends with his hero E. M. Forster and was hailed by Somerset Maugham. As an associate of Auden, Spender, C. Day Lewis, Louis MacNeice, John Lehmann, and Cyril Connolly, he became legendary as an intellectual leader of a new movement in English letters.

By collaborating with Auden on three avant-garde plays and by supporting various left-wing causes, Isherwood also gained a reputation for ideological commitment. But partly because of his growing awareness of himself as a homosexual, he deeply distrusted communism, and he became more and more dissatisfied with the emptiness of left-wing rhetoric.

In 1938, he published an early autobiography, *Lions and Shadows*, that explained—perhaps prophetically—his need to escape from England in order to mature. In the same year, he and Auden accepted a commission to write a travel book about the Far East. They decided to travel to China and report on the Chinese struggle against the Japanese invasion. On their return, they stopped briefly in New York. The results of this trip were the 1939 book *Journey to a War* and the fascination of both writers with America. During the political crises of late 1938, as the world teetered on the brink of global conflict, Isherwood became obsessed with the dread of war, and he found life in England intolerable.

In January 1939, when the political tension had calmed, Isherwood and Auden emigrated to the United States. Their decision reflected both their disenchantment with England and their loss of political faith. On board the ship bringing them to America, Isherwood realized that he was a pacifist, a conviction prompted by his fear that Heinz might be serving in the German army. When Auden and Isherwood arrived in New York, Auden almost immediately found the city stimulating and enjoyable, while Isherwood was overcome with despair, feeling a great emptiness within himself. At the invitation of the philosopher Gerald Heard, whom he had known in London, he and a young American lover named Vernon traveled to California. This trip too proved to be momentous, for he was to settle there permanently.

Soon after Isherwood's arrival in Los Angeles, Heard introduced him to Aldous Huxley and to Swami Prabhavananda, a Hindu monk of the Rama-krishna order who was head of the Vedanta Society of Southern California. Under the direction of Prabhavananda, Isherwood embraced Vedantism and seriously considered becoming a monk. His conversion after a long history of opposition to religion acknowledged a spiritual need that the narrowly moralistic Christianity of his youth could not satisfy.

In contrast to Christianity, Vedanta teaches that God dwells within man; it is nondogmatic; and it "does not emphasize the vileness of man's mortal nature or the enormity of sin."[2] More specifically, Vedanta does not arbitrarily distinguish between homosexuality and heterosexuality as obstacles to spiritual growth.

But quite apart from the sympathy Isherwood felt for Vedantic philosophy, his conversion was prompted by the personality of Prabhavananda,

who became his surrogate father. After coming to
know the guru, he gradually ceased to be an atheist
because he found himself unable to disbelieve in
Prabhavananda's belief in God. Describing the
guru-disciple relationship as "the center of everything that religion means to me," Isherwood declared that were he to be deprived of it, "then my
life would become a nightmare of guilt, boredom,
and self-disgust."[3] The importance of Isherwood's
conversion can hardly be overestimated, for all his
later work is informed by Vedantism.

In 1940, Isherwood accepted a job as a scriptwriter with Metro-Goldwyn-Mayer. From his Cambridge days, he had been interested in film, and he
had worked briefly in London as a scriptwriter, an
experience he was to recreate brilliantly in his first
novel written in America, *Prater Violet* (1945).
Since the early 1940s, Isherwood has often been
employed in the Hollywood motion picture industry, and many of his friends have been actors, ac-
tresses, scriptwriters, directors, and producers, including Charles Laughton, Greta Garbo, Berthold
Viertel, and Gavin Lambert. Other friends have included such luminaries from the worlds of music,
literature, and art as Igor Stravinsky, Tennessee
Williams, Gore Vidal, and David Hockney.

In 1941, Isherwood left MGM to work at a
Pennsylvania hostel for German refugees. Spon-
sored by the Quakers, the hostel was designed to
teach the refugees English and to help orient them
to American life. Isherwood's experience in Germany proved invaluable in this employment, and
he was later to use his observation of the Quakers as
a source for many scenes in his novel *The World in
the Evening*. In February of 1942, he registered as a
conscientious objector and volunteered for service
at a forestry fire-fighting camp near Santa Barbara,
California. Because the age limit for conscription

was lowered to thirty-eight in December, he was never called up for service as a fire fighter; but the experience of a friend, Denny Fouts, in a similar camp provided the source of important scenes in his novel *Down There on a Visit*.

Isherwood moved into the Vedanta monastery in Hollywood in 1943 and began collaborating with Swami Prabhavananda on a new translation of the Hindu holy book, the Bhagavad Gita. This was the first of several translations of Hindu religious works the two were to collaborate on over the next decade. In 1943, Isherwood also accepted the position of editor of *Vedanta and the West*, a journal published by the Vedanta Society to which Isherwood himself contributed essays. He was later to collect selected articles from the periodical for publication in book form, *Vedanta for the Western World* (1945) and *Vedanta for Modern Man* (1951), and to write a biography of Ramakrishna (1965) and a personal account of his religious experience, *An Approach to Vedanta* (1963).

Isherwood moved out of the monastery in 1945 and set up housekeeping with William Caskey, a handsome young Irishman from Kentucky; and in 1946, the novelist became a naturalized citizen of the United States, using the occasion to legalize his abandonment of his two middle names. In September of 1947, he and Caskey began a six-month tour of South America that resulted in the 1949 travel book, *The Condor and the Cows*, which was illustrated with Caskey's photographs. The Isherwood-Caskey relationship dissolved amicably in 1951, when Caskey embarked on a career as a merchant seaman.

The success of his friend and fellow Vedantist John van Druten's dramatic adaptation of the Berlin stories, *I Am a Camera*, improved Isherwood's financial position in 1951. At the end of that year, he visited England and Berlin, where he was briefly reunited with Heinz. Upon his return to California in April 1952, be began working on *The World in the Evening,* his first novel to employ an American setting. When this book was published in 1954, it sold well but disappointed many critics, some of whom concluded that Isherwood betrayed his early promise by emigrating to the United States.

In the winter of 1953, Isherwood fell in love with an eighteen-year-old college student, Don Bachardy. In February 1954, the two began living together. The discrepancy in their ages scandalized many of their friends, but the relationship has proved to be the most enduring union of Isherwood's life. Bachardy has since achieved independent success as an artist, and he and Isherwood have collaborated on a number of motion picture and television scripts and on a dramatization of Isherwood's 1967 novel, *A Meeting by the River.* At the conclusion of *Christopher and His Kind,* Isherwood describes Bachardy as "the ideal companion to whom you can reveal yourself totally and yet be loved for what you are, not for what you pretend to be."

Although Isherwood had previously rejected the idea of a teaching career, in 1959 he accepted an offer of a visiting professorship in the English department of California State College, Los Angeles. He taught there for two semesters and subsequently held similar appointments at various campuses of the University of California. His teaching experience proved a valuable source for the setting of his 1964 novel, *A Single Man.*

In the late 1950s and early 1960s, Isherwood worked on his biography of Ramakrishna and on the novel *Down There on a Visit* (1962). In late 1963, he accompanied Swami Prabhavananda to Calcutta, where a friend of theirs, John Yale, took final mo-

nastic vows, an experience Isherwood incorporated
as the central event of his ninth novel, *A Meeting by
the River*.

The success of *Down There on a Visit* caused
many critics to reconsider their premature dismissal
of Isherwood as a failed English writer who was unable to write successfully about the American experience. The even greater achievement of *A Single
Man* confirmed the novelist's deepening maturity,
and its brilliant depiction of Los Angeles testified to
his understanding of American life. The completeness of his transition from an English to an Anglo-
American writer may be indicated by the decision
to entitle his 1966 collection of fugitive articles, stories, and poems from the past *Exhumations*.

During the 1960s, Isherwood became interested in heredity as a key to his personality. When
his mother died in 1960, she left several volumes of
diaries that spanned most of her life and a packet of
letters her husband had written to her. Reading
over these diaries and letters, Isherwood became
convinced that his parents, his brother, and he were
all part of a single circuit. In 1968, he began work
on *Kathleen and Frank*, a biography of his parents
constructed from their diaries and letters. Pointing
the direction of his growing interest in autobiography, the book proved to be "chiefly about Christopher."

Published in late 1971, *Kathleen and Frank*
contained the casual but explicit revelation of
Isherwood's homosexuality. As part of the promo-
tional effort for the book, the author appeared on
several television interview programs in early 1972
and openly discussed his sexual orientation, explaining its centrality in his life. From that time on-
ward, he has been an active participant in the American gay liberation movement, frequently appearing

on behalf of the equal rights struggle at political rallies and fund-raising events.

The autobiographical impulse that prompted the shape of nearly all his novels and that had already yielded *Lions and Shadows* and *Kathleen and Frank* found its most sustained expression in the 1970s, when Isherwood became even more preoccupied with the pattern of his life. In 1976, he published *Christopher and His Kind*, a sexual and political autobiography that reinterprets his experiences in the 1930s from the perspective of the 1970s. Early in 1980, he published *My Guru and His Disciple*, a spiritual autobiography that recounts his relationship with Prabhavananda. His homosexuality and his religious commitment have been of overwhelming importance in his life and in his art, and it is appropriate that they are the subjects of his most recent books.

The decade of the 1970s solidified Isherwood's reputation as one of our most important living writers. A number of scholarly books and essays analyzed his novels, and his life became the subject of two biographies. In 1976 alone, an important scholarly journal, *Twentieth Century Literature*, devoted an entire issue to discussions of his works and he was featured in a major exhibit at London's National Portrait Gallery. The exhibit was entitled "Young Writers of the Thirties" and recognized Isherwood's status as a towering figure of that era. But perhaps the most significant critical trend of the 1970s was the rediscovery of his later work. During the decade, all of his novels were reprinted in widely available paperback editions.

Isherwood has repeatedly referred to life as an enormous journey that necessitates the crossing of various frontiers. On his own enormous journey, he has continually used his powers of observation and insight as aids in interpreting the significance of our shared trip toward a common destination. At the end of his most recent book, he writes that "my life is still beautiful to me—beautiful because of Don, because of the enduring fascination of my efforts to describe my life-experience in my writing, because of my interest in the various predicaments of my fellow-travellers on this journey. How I wish I were able to reassure them that all is ultimately well—particularly those who are quite certain that it isn't; that life is meaningless and unjust!" He adds that he cannot reassure his fellow-travelers because "I can't speak with the absolute authority of a knower."

But the integrity of his vision, the power of his art, and the example of the life from which that art is distilled ultimately reassure us all. Taken together they affirm the possibilities of honesty, courage, and commitment. As Carolyn Heilbrun notes, "His life has been a life of extraordinary adventure, accomplishment, and love: he seems to have meant much to many people."[4] Described by Gore Vidal as "the best prose writer in English,"[5] he is a masterful stylist, a subtle ironist, and a witty and compassionate moralist. Christopher Isherwood is among the century's most insightful observers of the human condition.

2

Elegies for a Dying City: The Berlin Stories

The Berlin stories established Isherwood's reputation as a major writer in the 1930s, and they remain his most popular work. In them, Isherwood masters a unique voice and point of view, creates some of the most memorable characters in modern fiction, and brilliantly depicts a city in the process of decaying from within. More than any other writer, Isherwood created the indelible picture of Berlin in the late 1920s and early 1930s.

Consisting of two novels, *The Last of Mr. Norris* and *Goodbye to Berlin,* the Berlin stories were originally intended to form part of what Isherwood projected as a "huge tightly constructed melodramatic novel" to be entitled *The Lost.* This title was chosen to suggest "not only The Astray and The Doomed—referring tragically to the political events in Germany and our epoch—but also 'The Lost' in quotation marks—referring satirically to those individuals whom respectable society shuns in horror. . . ."[1] Although Isherwood eventually abandoned his plan for an epic novel, in the Berlin stories he nevertheless achieves his goal of sketching simultaneously both a doomed underworld and a political tragedy.

The two novels are fundamentally political. Each is haunted by the brooding specter of Nazism, as Hitler's inexorable rise to power adds urgency and depth to the seemingly insignificant events of plots that focus on individuals at the periphery of the public arena. The chaotic political climate of Berlin in the early 1930s is both cause and effect of the paralyzing fatalism that afflicts almost all the characters in both novels. This fatalism mirrors political impotence and contributes to the conditions that make possible the success of fascism.

As an exploration of the way in which public and private concerns inevitably intersect, the Berlin stories are passionately engaged, and they capture the broad sweep of history. Yet they avoid overt political statements and obtrusive ideology, self-consciously domesticating the political tragedy that they document. As Paul Piazza remarks, the stories "achieve political significance not because of their ideological content, but because of their heightened sensitivity to the obscure dread, the vague, unnatural menace inherent in the last days of the Weimar Republic."[2]

This domestication of tragedy is one of Isherwood's supreme accomplishments in the Berlin stories, and it is achieved in a variety of distinct yet related ways. First of all, Isherwood's playful, seemingly artless and transparent prose flows so easily that it lulls the reader into a false sense of comprehension. Only after fully absorbing the smooth surface of the language is one startled into recognizing its emotional and ironic implications.

In *The Last of Mr. Norris,* Isherwood observes that in the Berlin of the early 1930s, "The murder reporters and the jazz-writers had inflated the German language beyond recall":

The vocabulary of newspaper invective (traitor, Versailles-lackey, murder-swine, Marx-crook, Hitler-swamp, Red-pest) had come to resemble through excessive use, the formal phraseology of politeness employed by the

Chinese. The word *Liebe,* soaring from the Goethe standard, was no longer worth a whore's kiss. *Spring, moonlight, youth, roses, girl, darling, heart, May:* such was the miserably devalued currency dealt in by the authors of all those tangoes, waltzes, and fox-trots which advocated the private escape.

Isherwood's style, with its simple diction, unemphatic stress, frequent anticlimaxes, and syntactic discontinuity, amounts to a kind of linguistic deflation intended to contrast with the empty rhetoric of propaganda and of escapism.[3]

Another way Isherwood domesticates political tragedy is by adopting E. M. Forster's "tea-tabling" method. As Isherwood writes in *Lions and Shadows,* quoting his friend Edward Upward, "The whole of Forster's technique is based on the tea-table: instead of trying to screw all his scenes up to the highest possible pitch, he tones them down until they sound like mothers'-meeting gossip. . . . In fact, there's actually *less* emphasis laid on the big scenes than on the unimportant ones: that's what's so utterly terrific." Thus in the Berlin stories, the Nazi menace looms in the background, only occasionally intruding into the action at the forefront; and the focus of each book moves with cinematic indiscrimination from one apparently unimportant detail to another.

Related to Isherwood's self-conscious strategy of understatement is his seemingly naive first-person narration. The narrators—William Bradshaw in *The Last of Mr. Norris* and Christopher Isherwood in *Goodbye to Berlin*—bear the author's own names, thus helping impart a semblance of autobiographical verisimilitude to the novels. But these narrators ought not be confused or equated with the author. They are, in fact, fictional personae. Their passivity, lack of commitment, and failure to perceive the irony of their relationships with the char-

acters in the books they narrate serve to distinguish
them from the author of those books, even as these
same qualities help make possible the tea-tabling of
public tragedy.

The moral and political points of view of the
Berlin stories emerge as a result of this disjunction
between the author and his namesake personae.
The narrator of *Goodbye to Berlin* describes himself as "a camera with its shutter open, quite passive, recording, not thinking. Recording the man
shaving at the window opposite and the woman in
the kimono washing her hair. Some day, all this will
have to be developed, carefully printed, fixed."
This paragraph, the most famous and most often
quoted passage in Isherwood's work, is important
not merely as a misleading description of narrative
technique. It is significant as well for the distinction it implies between the passive recorder's role
as camera and both the artist's responsibility to se-
lect what is to be recorded and the reader's duty to
interpret the significance of that selection.

Isherwood contrives to place his readers in po-
sitions of intellectual and moral superiority to his
likeable but neutral narrators. Their lack of sophisti-
cation both accounts for the novel's understatement
of political consciousness and forces the attentive
reader to discover political significance as a means
of compensating for their frequent lapses of perception. The reader's participation in the novels as a
more acute observer than the passive narrators
helps create the ironic perspective that is one of
Isherwood's most striking features.

And finally, the essentially comic mode of the
Berlin stories, especially *The Last of Mr. Norris* and
the "Sally Bowles" section of *Goodbye to Berlin*,
contributes to the domestication of tragedy. The
novels are inhabited by comic grotesques, who
thoroughly dominate the stories. The narrators fre-

quently translate what might appear shocking or lurid if told from a different point of view into comic
tableaux, as in the scenes revealing the sexual in-
dulgences of Arthur Norris or the pederastic fantasies of Baron von Pregnitz. Moreover, the comic
characters are frequently so charming as to be, at
least temporarily, immune to moral censure.

Although these characters are incapable of
arousing tragic emotions, they can and do stimulate
pathos. In fact, the very lightness of tone in which
the colorful grotesques are rendered intensifies the
pathos of their predicaments. The comic sensibility
that delights in the grotesquerie of Berlin in the
early 1930s also conveys the human vulnerability
beneath the exaggerated poses: the comedy is compassionate as well as farcical. Preeminently, however, the comedy of the Berlin stories is ironic, for
the comic figures and situations are placed in the
context of a public tragedy that finally colors every
action in the novels.

Ultimately, the public tragedy invests the
ironic comedy with an elegiac tone, a pervasive
sense of loss. The Berlin stories become elegies for
a dying city. Filtered through the sensibilities of repressed young Englishmen, vaguely in rebellion
against English hypocrisy and class consciousness,
the novels evoke a mythic Berlin of sexual and political freedom only to acknowledge the artificiality
of myth in the harsh light of reality. The city that
"glowed so brightly and invitingly in the night sky
above the plains" is finally exposed as "cold and
cruel and dead. Its warmth is an illusion, a mirage
of the winter desert."

The Last of Mr. Norris

The Last of Mr. Norris was first published in 1935
by Leonard and Virginia Woolf's Hogarth Press un-

der the title *Mr. Norris Changes Trains.* Its New
York publisher, William Morrow, somewhat dubi-
ously declared the British title obscure, so Isherwood altered it for the American edition. *The Last
of Mr. Norris,* he explains, is a title which "should
be followed by a very faint question mark."[4]

The novel opens in 1930 with William Bradshaw, a young English writer, en route to Berlin,
where he hopes to earn at least a marginal living as
an English-language tutor. On the train, he encounters Arthur Norris, a nervous, middle-aged Englishman wearing a faintly ridiculous wig. Later, in
Berlin, the two become fast friends. A small-time
crook living on his wits, a flagellant and boot fetish-
ist, Norris introduces Bradshaw to other members
of the Berlin demimonde: Olga, the procuress;
Anni, the prostitute, and her Communist boyfriend,
Otto; Baron von Pregnitz, a wealthy government official with pederastic fantasies; and—more sinis-
terly—Norris's secretary, Schmidt, a blackmailing
schemer who terrorizes his employer.

In the course of the book, Norris's fortunes fluc-
tuate widely, and he is finally reduced to renting a
room in Fräulein Schroeder's boardinghouse,
where Bradshaw also lives. It becomes clear that
Norris is an adventurer, using the political turmoil
of the time for his own ends. He joins the Communist party, then betrays it to the French Intelligence
Service; using Bradshaw as bait, he exposes von
Pregnitz to the bribery of the French and the black-
mail of Schmidt.

The novel ends in 1933. The Communist party
collapses, and its leader, Ludwig Bayer, is assassi-
nated; Hitler becomes chancellor; Baron von Pregnitz commits suicide; Otto only barely escapes arrest; Olga, Anni, Frl. Schroeder, and other Berliners
adapt to the altered political realities; and with the
aid of Bradshaw, Norris flees Germany, only to be

pursued relentlessly by Schmidt. In a letter to Bradshaw, Norris asks incredulously, "Tell me, William
... *what* have I done to deserve all this?"

The key to the novel's absorbing interest resides in the mysterious charm of Mr. Norris himself.
Among the most seductive comic figures in modern
literature, he is both lovable and dangerous. An in-
congruous combination of charm and guile, timidity
and boldness, Norris is romanticized by Bradshaw
as "a most amazing old crook." At the very beginning of the book, William recognizes him as "a
schoolboy surprised in the act of breaking one of the
rules" and describes his eyes as "innocently
naughty," crystallizing Norris's childlike capacity
for maintaining an air of innocence even when
guilty of private and public betrayal.

Norris's approach to life is primarily aesthetic.
Claiming membership in the Wildean Café Royale
literary circle, he is a caricature of the *fin de siècle*
aesthete, even to the point of echoing Wilde in his
rueful confession, "I put my genius into my life, not
into my art."[5] He reports his decision to join the
Communist party as an aesthetic judgment: injustice, he explains, "offends my sense of the beautiful." When summoned for questioning by the Political Police, he confides, "It's a curious fact that since
my earliest years, I have had an instinctive dislike
of the police. The very cut of their uniforms offends
me, and the German helmets are not only hideous
but somehow rather sinister."

For Norris, style triumphs over substance, appearances over reality. His personal appearance
quite literally represents an attempt to disguise reality. Possessing a number of "queerly cut" wigs
and addicted to an elaborate dressing-table ritual, at
which Bradshaw and Frl. Schroeder frequently as-
sist, Norris maintains an elegant, youthful appearance at odds with his actual circumstances. "He

might have been a popular actor," Bradshaw comments when he returns from a trip to the countryside and finds Norris "barbered, manicured, and perfumed," looking "positively younger." The deception of his personal appearance mirrors the evasiveness of his conversation and the treachery of his actions.

Even Norris's sexual tastes symbolize the preeminence of style in his life and give expression to his acting talent. Bradshaw's startling discovery of Norris in the throes of masochistic pleasure is wonderfully comic:

The first person I saw was Anni. She was standing in the middle of the room. Arthur cringed on the floor at her feet. He had removed several more of his garments, and was now dressed, lightly but with perfect decency, in a suit of mauve silk underwear, a rubber abdominal belt and a pair of socks. In one hand he held a brush and in the other a yellow shoe-rag. Olga towered behind him, brandishing a heavy leather whip.

"You call that clean, you swine!" she cried, in a terrible voice. "Do them again this minute! And if I find a speck of dirt on them I'll thrash you till you can't sit down for a week."

As she spoke she gave Arthur a smart cut across the buttocks. He uttered a squeal of pain and pleasure, and began to brush and polish Anni's boots with feverish haste.

The farcical quality of the scene results from the variance between the flat tone of the description and the heightened emotion inherent in the action described. The objectivity that isolates such realistic details as Arthur's "mauve silk underwear" and "rubber abdominal belt" and notes the color of the shoe-rag translates what is felt by the participants as feverish sexual fantasy into a ludicrous tableau.

But it is precisely the fantasy element in sadomasochism that is the most important aspect of

Norris's sexual eccentricity and that makes this comic scene a serious parody of the coming political disruption in the novel. When Norris is summoned for questioning by the Political Police and fears that he may actually be tortured, William, only half facetiously, asks, "wouldn't you rather enjoy it?" In reply, Arthur giggles, "Well, well, perhaps if the examination were to be conducted by Frl. Anni, or some equally charming young lady, I might undergo it with—er—very mixed feelings." Norris's real fear of actual torture by the police underlines the fact that his revelry in the simulated punishment of sadomasochistic games depends on a discrepancy between fantasy and reality. But in *The Last of Mr. Norris* reality gradually intrudes into fantasy, and the make-believe torturers are finally replaced by a truly sadistic political regime.

Similarly, the public world gradually intrudes into the private lives of all the characters in the novel. At the beginning of the book, attention is almost exclusively centered on the personal relationships and private eccentricities of the characters. But as the plot mounts in intensity, as the calm of 1930 develops into the civil disturbances of the winter of 1931-32, when "Hate exploded suddenly, without warning, out of nowhere; at street corners, in restaurants, cinemas, dance halls, swimming baths; at midnight, after breakfast, in the middle of the afternoon," the novel increasingly focuses on political events, and the public and the private spheres become inextricably linked. Concurrently, the comic tone modulates into grimly ironic seriousness.

This intersection of the private and the public is prefigured quite early in the novel, however. On his first visit to Arthur's flat, Bradshaw notices that there are two front doors, each with its own nameplate. These nameplates, "Arthur Norris. Private" and "Arthur Norris. Import and Export," imply a neat separation of an individual's public and private lives. But when the door is opened, William discovers that "the Private side of the entrance hall was divided from the Export side only by a thick hanging curtain." In fact, there is no barrier at all between Norris's public and private lives, for all of his actions are selfishly motivated, and his political treachery is a personal betrayal as well as a public one.

Even Norris's selfishness is politically significant, and what at first appears comic is retrospectively revealed as ironic. For example, Norris early in the novel explains his personal philosophy to William: "I do and always shall maintain that it is the privilege of the richer, but less mentally endowed members of the community to contribute to the upkeep of people like myself." In its immediate context, this statement appears merely comic, perfectly consistent with the waggish aesthete's exclusively subjective view of the world. But by the end of the novel, this personal credo comes to be recognized as a grotesque parody of both the Nazi *Übermensch* mentality and the Communist goal of redistributing wealth from those of the greatest ability to those of the greatest need.

The impossibility of separating the private and the public is illustrated most poignantly in the case of Baron von Pregnitz, the character who attempts most honestly to achieve such separation. A prominent politician and a homosexual whose secret fantasies revolve around English schoolboy adventure stories, he at first seems to have succeeded in compartmentalizing the two distinct areas of his life. But the necessity of separating his personal life from his political role itself indicates the intrusion of the public into the private.

Moreover, the strain of leading a divided life

proves greater than he thought it would, as William notes when he visits von Pregnitz soon after the baron's appointment to the cabinet:

He was sentimental and preoccupied by turns. The intrigues which were going on within the Cabinet probably caused him a good deal of worry. And he regretted the freedom of his earlier bohemian existence. His public responsibilities debarred him from the society of the young men I had met at his Mecklenburg villa. Only their photographs remained to console him now, bound in a sumptuous album which he kept locked away in an obscure cupboard.

The growing power of the virulently antihomosexual Nazis renders von Pregnitz increasingly vulnerable. Ultimately his public and private worlds are horribly united when he is blackmailed by Schmidt, agrees to sell information to the French, is discovered by the police, and pathetically commits suicide in a public lavatory.

Even the single character who is exclusively defined as a public figure, Ludwig Bayer, the Communist leader, initially accepts a distinction between public and private roles. When he exposes Norris's treachery to Bradshaw, he adds, "Norris is your friend, I know. Mind, I have not said this against him as a man; the private life is not our concern." In many ways the most attractive of all the characters in *The Last of Mr. Norris,* Bayer is fatally mistaken in his assumption that the private life does not impinge on the public. Telling William, "I think that now you will be more careful with whom you make a friend," he inadvertently acknowledges his error. Significantly, the ugly report of his murder in the Spandau barracks includes an incongruously personal detail—"his left ear was torn right off"— powerfully summarizing the conjunction of the public and the private in the Nazi terror.

The Nazi terror tangles the private and public lives of even the most minor and least politically sophisticated characters in the novel. After the Reichstag fire early in 1933, Frl. Schroeder helps Bradshaw hide his copy of the *Communist Manifesto* and other incriminating papers in anticipation of house searches, a procedure that vividly symbolizes the general invasion of the private realm by public power. Otto only barely escapes arrest by Werner Baldow, his Nazi rival for the private charms of Anni. As Otto comments, "There's lots of old scores being paid off nowadays." Bradshaw's friend Fritz Wendel injures his arm in an automobile accident wholly unrelated to the political unrest; as a consequence, however, "he wouldn't venture out of doors. Bandages of any kind gave rise to misunderstandings, especially when, like Fritz, you had a dark complexion and coal-black hair." Most revoltingly, the insensitive journalist Helen Pratt uses the political chaos as an opportunity for personal advancement.

In a masterfully crafted description of the reaction of most Berliners to Hitler's elevation to the chancellorship in 1933, Isherwood mixes the mundane and the ominous to sketch the complex combination of public issues and private prejudices that contributed to Hitler's success:

Our street looked quite gay when you turned into it and saw the black-white-red flags hanging motionless from windows against the blue spring sky. On the Nollendorfplatz people were sitting out of doors before the café in their overcoats, reading about the coup d'état in Bavaria. Goring spoke from the radio horn at the corner. Germany is awake, he said. An ice-cream shop was open. Uniformed Nazis strode hither and thither, with serious, set faces, as though on weighty errands. The newspaper readers by the café turned their heads to watch them pass and smiled and seemed pleased.

They smiled approvingly at these youngsters in their big, swaggering boots who were going to upset the Treaty of Versailles. They were pleased because it would soon be summer, because Hitler had promised to protect the small tradesmen, because their newspapers told them that the good times were coming. They were suddenly proud of being blond. And they thrilled with a furtive, sensual pleasure, like schoolboys, because the Jews, their business rivals, and the Marxists, a vaguely defined minority of people who didn't concern them, had been satisfactorily found guilty of the defeat and the inflation, and were going to catch it.

The world described here is one in which the public and the private, the political and the personal, have become so completely merged that distinctions between them are meaningless.

Bradshaw's inability to understand the connection between the public and the private constitutes his most serious flaw of perception, and this failure is a direct result of his naively nonjudgmental detachment, the very quality that makes him such a personable and trustworthy narrator. His refusal to condemn Norris—his continuing susceptibility to Norris's charm and his persistent regard of Norris as essentially an innocent but naughty child even in the face of contrary evidence—reflects his belief that personal relationships can be rigidly separated from political ones. But his detachment finally comes to be seen as paradigmatic of the private failures that lead to public consequences. For although he is uncommitted to any political cause, William—albeit innocently and unknowingly—is nevertheless manipulated by Norris and thus implicated in the personal and political treachery that culminates in von Pregnitz's suicide and the Communist collapse.

William's bemused detachment melts at only two points in the novel. They are important, for in both cases the political and the personal briefly merge in his consciousness. Unfortunately, however, in each instance the merger is only temporary, and personal preoccupations eventually supplant the incipient political awareness. Ironically, in the world of Berlin in the early 1930s, the denial of political commitments is perforce itself a political stance.

The first time William abandons his detachment occurs when, after receiving the astonishing news of Norris's conversion to the Communist party, he agrees to accompany the unlikely, self-indulgent, luxury-loving convert to a party meeting. In his description of the workers' response to Ludwig Bayer, William suddenly departs from voyeurism and contrasts his own lack of commitment with the zeal of the Communists: "Their passion, their strength of purpose elated me. I stood outside it. One day, perhaps, I should be with it, but never of it. At present I just sat there, a half-hearted renegade from my own class, my feelings muddled by anarchism talked at Cambridge, by slogans from the confirmation service, by the tunes the band played when my father's regiment marched to the railway station, seventeen years ago." Bradshaw here criticizes his own passivity, but ultimately he remains the outsider. Even while admiring the party's communal spirit, his reactions reflect private rather than public needs.

The other point at which he abandons his detachment occurs when he learns how Norris misused him and betrayed the party. Bradshaw's political consciousness is so underdeveloped in comparison to his personal affection for Norris that he forgives the rogue, even while fully appreciating the absurdity of his own gullibility. With disarming disingenuousness, Norris tells him, "If my behavior hasn't always been consistent, I can truly say that I

am and always shall be loyal to the Party, at heart."
In response, William muses: "He was outrageous,
grotesque, utterly without shame. But what was I to
answer? At that moment, had he demanded it, I'd
have sworn that two and two make five."

Bradshaw's gullibility is also revealed in his
failure to recognize in Schmidt the ugly mirror of
Norris's own reality, the reality disguised by
Norris's cosmetics and personal charm. The sinister
Schmidt is the one character William unequivocally
condemns, yet the secretary functions in the novel
as Norris's Jungian "shadow figure," the negative
reflection of his personality.[6] Schmidt has no independent existence; "he had made his master's interests identical with his own." He is Norris's "right
hand," less suave and more brutal in his methods
but not different in kind.

Appropriately, by the end of the novel Schmidt
has quite literally become Norris's shadow. In a letter to Bradshaw, Arthur remarks that he and
Schmidt are "doomed to walk the Earth together."
This phrase—an unconscious allusion to Amos 3:3,
where a retributive Jehovah reproves the sins of Is-
rael by asking, "Can two walk together, except they
be agreed?"—seals the identification of Norris and
Schmidt. The two travel together from the Paradise
of California to the Purgatory of Mexico to the In-
ferno of South America, a journey the direction of
which is charted as certainly by the metaphors as by
the geography.

Much of the novel's irony pivots on William's
naiveté. He never seems fully to grasp the political
lessons implicit in the story he narrates. Those lessons are most apparent in Norris's disingenuous
comments in the letters that conclude the book. Referring to Hitler, he observes, "It is indeed tragic to
see how, even in these days, a *clever* and *unscrupulous liar* can deceive millions." In another letter, he

describes the Nazis as "nothing more or less than *criminals.*"

Although William fails to understand it, Isherwood's point is clear: Norris, himself a clever and unscrupulous liar, nothing more or less than a criminal, is actually a small-scale, comic version of Hitler. Just as his sadomasochistic pleasures parody the real sadism of the Nazi regime, so his (and his shadow Schmidt's) minor intrigues parody the major betrayals of Hitler, who is himself a split personality. The irony is that William's uncritical affection for the lovable rogue, an affection that readers unavoidably share for much of the novel, suddenly becomes analogous to the average German's political enthusiasm for Hitler. Private failures, including failures of commitment and perception, inevitably yield public consequences.

Significantly, the novel implicates the audience in its irony. The attentive reader ultimately corrects William's misperceptions and gullibility, but only after having fallen prey to the identical misjudgments. Arthur Norris is an endearing figure, and his charm does, for a while, insulate him from moral censure. The reader's recognition of William's errors of judgment is simultaneously a recognition of his or her own error, both in the past and potentially in the future. The effect of the book's irony is not only to condemn William's naiveté and passivity but also to force the reader toward compassionate understanding, both for William and for the German people.

The Last of Mr. Norris is, thus, a moral fable couched in comic form. The "very faint question mark" that is to be understood as following the title amounts to a serious political warning. But the miracle of the novel is that the comic tone intensifies the seriousness of the fable, while the political lesson is actually strengthened by the indirection of its

statement. *The Last of Mr. Norris* balances comic
and tragic perspectives, ultimately subsuming both
in an all-encompassing irony that embraces characters, narrator, and readers alike.

Goodbye to Berlin

Goodbye to Berlin was published in final form by
the Hogarth Press in 1939. Although sections of it
had appeared earlier in John Lehmann's influential
literary journal *New Writing* and in the Hogarth
Press's separately issued novella *Sally Bowles* of
1937, *Goodbye to Berlin* is not merely a collection
of previously published material. A brilliantly exe-
cuted and unified novel, its whole is far greater than
the sum of its parts.

The book opens with "A Berlin Diary (Autumn
1930)," which introduces the introspective narrator,
a young writer named Christopher Isherwood; his
fellow inhabitants of Frl. Schroeder's boardinghouse; and his pupil Hippi Bernstein and her family. In the "Sally Bowles" section that follows, Chris
becomes peripherally involved with the adventures
of an innocently naughty cabaret singer. Like Chris
an English expatriate, Sally delights in flouting
middle-class conventions, but she is frequently vic-
timized by others and is finally duped by a sixteen-
year-old con man.

The third section, "On Ruegen Island," recounts the summer of 1931, which Chris spends at a
seaside resort with Peter Wilkinson, an intellectual
English homosexual, and Otto Nowak, a young German working-class hustler. In the fourth section,
"The Nowaks," temporary financial hardship forces
Chris to join Otto and his family in an apartment in
the poorest section of Berlin. The family, consisting
of Otto, his tubercular mother, alcoholic father, list-

less sister Grete, and Nazi brother Lothar, finally disintegrates from the pressures of poverty and illness when Frau Nowak enters a sanatorium.

"The Landauers" traces Chris's relationship with a wealthy Jewish family, owners of a large department store. Tutor to their eighteen-year-old daughter, Natalia, Chris becomes fascinated with her enigmatic cousin Bernhard. Cloaked in a kind of Oriental mystery, Bernhard understands the coming political dislocation, but finds himself powerless to act effectively to save himself. At the end of the section, Chris learns that he has been killed. The novel concludes with "A Berlin Diary (Winter 1932–3)," in which the political crisis dominates. "The sun shines, and Hitler is master of this city," Chris writes, and concludes: "Even now I can't altogether believe that any of this has really happened."

Although Isherwood has described *Goodbye to Berlin* as a "loosely connected sequence of diaries and sketches,"[7] the description fails to do justice to the artful symmetry of the book. It achieves unity as a result of two structural principles. One involves the deliberate balancing of economic, sexual, cultural, and political polarities in the various sections and among the disparate characters, and the subsequent recognition of sameness underlying the diversity. For example, the crushing poverty of "The Nowaks" is contrasted with the guilt-inducing wealth of "The Landauers"; the aggressive heterosexuality of "Sally Bowles" is juxtaposed to the spoiled homosexual idyll of "On Ruegen Island"; the naive diary of 1930 is symmetrically balanced by the despairing one of 1932-33.

Moreover, characters are opposed to polar characters both within their own sections and across sectional divisions: the cerebral Englishman Peter Wilkinson and the physical German Otto Nowak;

the rebellious gentile Sally Bowles and the proper
Jewess Natalia Landauer; the Nazi youths and doctor in "On Ruegen Island" and the Communist boys
and scoutmaster in the concluding diary. But beneath these polarities of rich and poor, homosexual
and heterosexual, Jew and gentile, Communist and
Nazi is a shared reality of the deadened spirit that
unites everyone in the book, even as it makes any
real integration impossible.

The other source of unity is the continuing and
developing presence of the first-person narrator,
"Herr Issyvoo" as Frl. Schroeder calls him, "Chris"
as he is referred to by Sally. Isherwood has used the
term "dynamic portrait" to refer to certain of his
novels,[8] and the term is especially appropriate to
Goodbye to Berlin, for the novel is a complex, ever
deepening portrait of its narrator.

Although he becomes considerably more per-
ceptive than William Bradshaw, the narrator of
Goodbye to Berlin resembles him in his naiveté
and impassivity. They are both spectators rather
than participants. But whereas Bradshaw is essentially a static character, Chris has at least the capacity for growth; and whereas William's position as
passive reporter functions primarily to establish
ironic perspective in *The Last of Mr. Norris,* Chris's
passivity more complexly articulates theme and
heightens affective tone in *Goodbye to Berlin.*

The tone of the book as a whole, far more serious than that of *The Last of Mr. Norris,* is set early
in the opening diary, when Chris hears young men
whistling for their girls in the street below his window:

Their signals echo down the deep hollow street, lasciv-
ious and private and sad. Because of the whistling, I do
not care to stay here in the evenings. It reminds me that I
am in a foreign city, alone, far from home. Sometimes I

determine not to listen to it, pick up a book, try to read.
But soon a call is sure to sound, so piercing, so insistent,
so despairingly human, that at last I have to get up and
peep through the slats of the venetian blind to make quite
sure that it is not—as I know very well it could not possibly be—for me.

The plaintive note of frustrated isolation struck here
is never far beneath the surface of *Goodbye to
Berlin*. Even the forced gaiety of Sally Bowles rings
hollow, for it is a mask that never quite succeeds in
disguising the loneliness she shares with everyone
else in the book.

The essential loneliness of the human condition is, in fact, the major theme of *Goodbye to
Berlin*. All of its characters are isolated, imprisoned
within themselves, unable to establish fulfilling relationships with others. The promiscuity of Sally,
the neurotic willfulness of Peter, the selfishness of
Otto, and the paralyzing withdrawal of Bernhard
are all symptomatic of the loneliness that infects the
whole city. Chris's loneliness is most obvious of all,
expressed both in his poignant need to imagine that
someone whistles for him and in his persistent singleness throughout the book. The very structure of
the novel is a solipsistic circle tracing Chris's failure
to achieve intimacy. The book opens and closes
with a diary, the loneliest of literary forms.

Chris's singleness is emphasized by his open
sympathy for and his accessibility to all of the polar-
ized characters and by his inability to connect with
any of them except on superficial levels. In the
"Sally Bowles" section, he functions as a kind of big
brother to Sally, who tells him, "I'm glad you're not
in love with me, because, somehow, I couldn't possibly be in love with you." Although Frl. Schroeder
thinks of the two as an ideal couple, Chris is only
the pretended father of Sally's aborted child. Her
confidant and co-conspirator in her adventure with

the American millionaire Clive, he nevertheless remains an outsider. When Clive proposes that the three of them leave Berlin together, Chris envisions himself as the eternal third wheel: "Once started, we should never go back. We could never leave him. Sally, of course, he would marry. I should occupy an ill-defined position: a kind of private secretary without duties."

He is similarly the third wheel in "On Ruegen Island," sharing a beach house with Peter and Otto, incessantly analyzing their relationship, receiving the confidences of each, yet ultimately refusing to become involved. Peter tells him, "You're quite an ascetic . . . always withdrawing for your contemplations." When Otto returns to Berlin and Peter embarks for England, Chris refers to Otto's admirers, who used to gather in the evening outside the cabin, and remarks facetiously, "I shall have to go down and console them." It is the facetiousness of the comment that is most revealing. Left alone in the house he shared with the unhappy lovers, Chris suddenly finds the place lonely: "I miss Peter and Otto, and their daily quarrels, far more than I should have expected. And now even Otto's dancing partners have stopped lingering sadly in the twilight, under my window."

In "The Nowaks," Chris shares a bedroom with Otto, for whom he has an unstated but clearly implied sexual attraction, yet his only human contact occurs on his harrowing visit to Frau Nowak in the sanatorium, when he accepts the embrace of a sex-starved, desperately lonely patient: "My mouth pressed against Erna's hot, dry lips. I had no particular sensation of contact." Describing himself as Chris's "loving friend," Otto initiates the Englishman's decision to board with his family; and throughout the section, he flirts with Chris, frequently flexing his muscles for his friend's admiration. But although Chris appreciates the young German's "naked brown body so sleek with health," when Otto pleads, "Take me with you, Christoph," he responds, "I'm afraid you're a luxury I can't afford."

In "The Landauers," Chris repulses the advances of both Natalia and Bernhard. Natalia attempts to break through Chris's pleasant facade of social banalities and engage his true convictions. "I am afraid," she tells him, "you are vairy insincere. You do not give your real meaning." To this accusation, he replies, "Why should I? Arguments bore me." Chris arranges a disastrous meeting of Natalia and Sally, which effectively destroys his relationship with the former, for he allows her to believe that Sally is his lover. After the debacle, he reflects: "I didn't flatter myself that Natalia had ever wanted me as a lover, but she had certainly begun to behave towards me as a kind of bossy elder sister, and it was just this role—absurdly enough—which Sally had stolen from her." Rationalizing his conduct, he adds: "No, it was a pity, but on the whole, I decided, things were better as they were."

Chris's relationship with the enigmatic Bernhard is one of the most fascinating features of the novel. Chris finds him attractive and charming, yet remote and arrogant. "He is not going to tell me what he is really thinking or feeling," Chris declares, "and he despises me because I do not know." Like the Nazi doctor in "On Ruegen Island," Bernhard believes in discipline, but "for myself, not necessarily for others." He may be a severely repressed homosexual, and his attempts to reach out to Chris may represent a desperate struggle to escape the solitariness of his repression.

When Bernhard brings Chris to his family's country estate and tells him the painful story of his mother's unhappiness and suicide, he suddenly reacts against Chris's polite passivity and exclaims: "It disgusts your English public-school training, a little—this Jewish emotionalism." He describes his attempt at intimacy with Chris as "an experiment upon myself," explaining that for ten years, "I have never spoken intimately, as I have spoken to you, to-night, to any human soul." Later he proposes that he and Chris leave Berlin together, on condition that they do it that very night. Chris refuses, treating the proposal as a joke; but later he recognizes it "as Bernhard's last, most daring and most cynical experiment upon us both. For now I am certain—absolutely convinced—that his offer was perfectly serious."

At the end of the novel, Chris recognizes the limitations of his passivity and the consequences of the failure of engagement. But his inability to connect meaningfully even with the characters with whom he is in most intimate contact mirrors the state of Berlin itself. His personal failure is symptomatic of the social disease that blights the whole city and that culminates in the spiritual death represented by Hitler's eventual triumph. At the beginning of the final diary, Chris writes, "Berlin is a skeleton which aches in the cold: it is my own skeleton aching." The disease that leads to the city's death is seen in microcosm in all the characters, each of whom suffers from physical or mental maladies, and in the novel's brilliantly woven texture of allusions to disease and death.

The diseases from which the characters suffer range in seriousness from Natalia's pathological fastidiousness to Frau Nowak's tuberculosis, from Peter's neurosis to Bernhard's suicidal alienation. But though these illnesses frequently have physical manifestations, they are all spiritual at base. In *Lions and Shadows,* Isherwood recounts how, in the 1920s, he and Auden came under the influence

of the American psychologist Homer Lane, who be-
lieved that "diseases are . . . only warning symp-
toms of a sickness in the soul." The soul sickness of
Berlin is reflected in the hysteria that permeates almost every aspect of German society, from the Nowaks' domestic squabbles to the Berlin cathedral,
"which betrays, in its architecture, a flash of that
hysteria which flickers always behind every grave,
grey Prussian facade" and which Chris suggests
ought to be renamed the Church of the Immaculate
Consumption.

Homer Lane defined the disease of the soul as
the denial of the "Tree of Life." This denial is expressed most vividly in the novel by the incidental
portrait of a cocaine addict who "had a nervous tic
and kept shaking his head all the time, as if saying
to Life: No. No. No." But the denial of life may also
be seen in the recurrent images of distortion and
deception in which almost all aspects of Berlin society are depicted and in the air of unreality that pervades the novel.

In Berlin, appearances nearly always belie reality. Even the Salome bar, with its "stage lesbians
and some young men with plucked eyebrows," is
not genuine: "The management run it entirely for
the benefit of provincial sightseers." The camarade-
rie of the Communist dive Chris and Fritz Wendel
visit is "thoroughly sham." The genteel garden
party at Bernhard's villa on the evening of what
might have been a crucial election is "the dress-re-
hearsal of a disaster." Berlin itself is a "mirage of the
winter desert."

This distortion of reality is manifested most
poignantly in the hallucinations that afflict almost
all the characters. Peter suffers from paranoia and
hypochondria. Otto has a recurrent vision of a great
black hand, the next appearance of which, he
thinks, will signify his death. Sally fantasizes about

her lost baby. At the sanatorium, Chris momentarily loses touch with the phenomenal world, as the patients suddenly seem like ghosts, "a gang of terrifyingly soft muffled shapes—clawing us from our seats, dragging us hungrily down, in dead silence." And Bernhard suffers from the most severe dislocation of all: "an unpleasant feeling, such as one has in a dream, that I myself do not exist." These hallucinations, all of which are associated with death, represent the fatalistic denials of reality and of responsibility that lead to the fascist nightmare.

The importance of the hallucinations may be illuminated by Freud's *Beyond the Pleasure Principle*, the book Chris reads in "On Ruegen Island." In this monograph, Freud contrasts the pleasure principle with the reality principle. The former may be defined as unconscious, primitive instincts, which seek gratification regardless of social consequences. The reality principle imposes constraints on the pleasure principle or modifies it into socially acceptable forms. When individuals are dominated by the pleasure principle, Freud writes, "The fulfillment of wishes . . . is brought about in a hallucinatory manner by dreams."[9] Since almost all the characters in *Goodbye to Berlin* may be regarded as, in varying degrees, dominated by the pleasure principle, their hallucinations may reflect their innermost desires, however horrible these may appear to their conscious minds. And in a broader application, the hysteria of German society may itself be a hallucinatory death wish fulfilled in the Nazi terror.

Significantly, the novel's air of unreality encompasses as well the characters' determined obliviousness to politics. This obliviousness is particularly remarkable inasmuch as the political situation eventually affects the lives of all of them. Although anticipated in the opening diary in Frl. Mayr's anti-Semitism and in Herr Bernstein's grim jokes, the

political upheaval only gradually assumes importance, coming to the fore first in "The Landauers"
and most completely in the final diary. Yet it is always hovering in the background, even impinging
on Sally with the collapse of the Darmstädter und
National Bank.

But for most of the characters, as for Hippi
Bernstein, who refers to the political situation "with
a conventional melancholy, as when one speaks of
religion," politics are "quite unreal." Although one
of their sons is a serious Nazi and the other a
feigned Communist, the senior Nowaks' political
awareness consists only of his slogan "we're all
equal as God made us" and her naive question
"why can't we have the Kaiser back?" Even to
Bernhard, who is politically aware, "all this seems
to me a little unreal, a little . . . trivial."

As late as the final diary, Berliners do not take
the expanding fascist movement seriously. When a
fistfight breaks out between two Jews and a Nazi
and when storm troopers stab a youth on the street,
the citizens shake their heads and murmur "Al-
lerhand!" The Nazi demonstration and Communist
counterdemonstration at the Bülowplatz is regarded
as "too much like a naughty schoolboy's game to be
seriously alarming." When Hitler forms a cabinet,
"Nobody thinks it can last till the spring." One consequence of this unreality is strikingly indicated
when Chris describes his handsome young friend
Rudi's adventures in the Communist youth organization as a "make-believe story-book game." He
adds: "The Nazis will play it with him. The Nazis
won't laugh at him; they'll take him on trust for
what he pretended to be."

The refusal to take politics seriously is itself as
much a symptom of the soul sickness that denies the
"Tree of Life" as is the overwhelming loneliness in
the city. Bernhard's self-deprecating incapacity to

believe in the importance of his own life leads literally to his death at the hands of the fascists. But the
failure of involvement is shared by all the characters in *Goodbye to Berlin* and eventually leads to
the spiritual death of the city itself.

The relationship between the failure of engagement and the death of the city is expressed most
clearly when Sally, Chris, and Clive, discussing
their plans to leave Berlin, suddenly notice "a most
elegant funeral" passing below Clive's hotel window. It is the funeral of Hermann Müller, the inef-
fectual leader of the centrist coalition, whose death
symbolizes, as Alan Wilde points out, "the fact that
German democracy is dying."[10] As "the pale stead-
fast clerks, government officials, trade union secre-
taries—the whole drab weary pageant of Prussian
Social Democracy—trudged past under their banners towards the silhouetted arches of the Branden-
burg Tor," Sally notices only the marvelous sunset.
Chris comments: "She was quite right. We had
nothing to do with those Germans down there,
marching, or with the dead man in the coffin, or
with the words on the banners." This separation
from common humanity is part of the universal hallucination that denies life.

In the course of the novel, Chris's political
awareness deepens. He comes to realize, for instance, the harrowing fate in store for German Jews.
As he observes the election party at Bernhard's
villa, he remarks with fatefully accurate foresight,
"However often the decision may be delayed, all
these people are ultimately doomed." Later he
warns Bernhard, "The Nazis may write like schoolboys, but they're capable of anything. That's just
why they're so dangerous. People laugh at them,
right up to the last moment."

The city's soul sickness, its failure of commitment to life, finally dooms nearly all Berliners. Cap-

italist and worker, Communist and Nazi, homosexual and heterosexual, gentile and Jew: almost all the characters are fated to suffer—in varying degrees—the physical and spiritual agony in store for Berlin. Frl. Schroeder, who had voted Communist in November, begins to speak reverently of "Der Führer" in May. "She is merely acclimatizing herself in accordance with a natural law, like an animal which changes its coat for the winter," Chris observes regretfully, rather than accusatorily. "Thousands of people like Frl. Schroeder are acclimatizing themselves," he adds. "After all, whatever government is in power, they are doomed to live in this town."

Some characters do escape the dying city, however, and their redemption is instructive, for it illustrates the values that might have saved Berlin. Peter and Sally leave Germany early in the book, and their escape is expedited by the fact that they are foreigners. But Peter's determination "to keep traveling until I'm clear of this bloody country" and to seek psychological help in England may be a sign of life and may represent a healthy instinct for self-preservation. Sally's dogged vitality, her emotional vulnerability, her failure to learn from hard experience, her continuing willingness to commit herself—illustrated most hilariously in her victimization by the sixteen-year-old "loony"—are all indications of an essential innocence.[11] Behind her brittle facade lurks a triumphantly human spirit.

Natalia's redemption is less ambiguous and more instructive. She escapes to Paris, where she pursues an art career. When she reappears near the end of the novel, everything about her is changed. Chris notes that "there was a dreamy, delighted smile upon her face" and realizes that she is in love. He learns that she is engaged to a physician. The love and the commitment represented by her en-

gagement and her career—as well as the symbolic
significance of her fiancé's profession—are values
that might have cured the soul sickness of the dying
city.

   Goodbye to Berlin ends in early spring of 1933.
In the remarkable final entry of his diary, Chris reveals the extent of the growth of his own perception
during the course of the book:

To-day the sun is brilliantly shining; it is quite mild and
warm. I go out for my last morning walk, without an over-
coat or hat. The sun shines, and Hitler is master of the
city. The sun shines, and dozens of my friends . . . are in
prison, possibly dead. . . . Perhaps at this very moment
Rudi is being tortured to death.
   I catch sight of my face in the mirror of a shop, and am
shocked to see that I am smiling. You can't help smiling,
in such beautiful weather. The trams are going up and
down the Kleiststrasse, just as usual. They and the people
on the pavement, and the teacosy dome of the Nollendorfplatz station have an air of curious familiarity, of striking
resemblance to something one remembers as normal and
pleasant in the past—like a very good photograph.

   As always, the external appearance of Berlin
disguises the reality within, but now the narrator
knows the difference between the two. As a consequence, in his recognition of the inadequacy of the
"very good photograph," Chris acknowledges the
limitations of the method he embraced at the beginning of the novel. To be "a camera with its shutter
open, quite passive, recording not thinking" is itself
to distort reality. In the spiritually dead city of 1933,
"the camera eye can document . . . the apparent
city, smiling in the sun," as Samuel Hynes explains,
"but it cannot record possible death or terror, or the
reality of evil."[12]
   Chris's recognition of the limitations of his passivity marks a crucial stage in the deepening por-

trait of him that the book provides. But Isherwood the novelist has known the lesson all along. His complex achievement in *Goodbye to Berlin* is to expose the discrepancy between the apparent and the real and to locate the source of the Nazi nightmare in the soul sickness that afflicts an entire society, while simultaneously painting a "dynamic portrait" of a young man coming of age. A book of haunting loneliness, *Goodbye to Berlin* is a masterful study of an inhibited young man, preoccupied with the ghosts of the past and the fears of the future, belatedly maturing in a world that is dying. The title's farewell is a valediction to youth as well as to a city.

But the novel is more than a character portrait set in a period of turbulent history. It is also a political study. Private loneliness and individual failures of involvement, personal isolation and particular distortions of reality all contribute to the public tragedy of fascism. The deadness of spirit so manifest in private relationships culminates in the spiritual death of a city smiling beneath the spring sun, outwardly warm and inviting, but inwardly cold and cruel. Containing no public figures and no obtrusive ideology, *Goodbye to Berlin* is among the most significant political novels of the twentieth century. It explores with startling insight and prophetic accuracy the most important political event of its time; and by recognizing that personal emotions of love and hate, commitment and passivity are also political emotions, it translates immediate political questions into enduring art.

The Berlin stories are elegies for a dying city. Compassionate rather than accusatory, understated rather than strident, the novels record the decline of the Weimar Republic by focusing on social and political outcasts. Depicting Berlin in all its squalor and poverty, loneliness and despair, they capture the fullness of a society on the brink of disaster. Isherwood, "more than any German writer," according to the German cultural historian Otto Friedrich, created the "matchless portrait of the city."[13] The Berlin of Herr Issyvoo, Frl. Schroeder, Sally Bowles, Baron von Pregnitz, Natalia and Bernhard Landauer, Otto Nowak, and Mr. Norris has been extended, in altered—often distorted—form, into the popular imagination through the adaptations of John van Druten in the 1951 play and 1955 film *I Am a Camera* and of John Kander and Fred Ebb in their 1966 musical and 1972 film *Cabaret.* But Isherwood's original Berlin stories remain, in Carolyn Heilbrun's words, "the best rendering we have of early Hitler Germany: an artistic re-creation of a society's self-betrayal."[14]

3

~~~~~~

Evil Mothers
and Truly Weak Men:
All the Conspirators,
The Memorial,
Collaborations with Auden

Isherwood's status as a major writer in the 1930s
rests not only on the Berlin stories but also on two
youthful novels and on three plays and a travel book
written in collaboration with W. H. Auden. One of
the novels, *The Memorial,* combines assured technique and mature vision and ranks among Isherwood's most successful books. In contrast, the
Auden-Isherwood plays succeed only intermittently. But *Journey to a War,* the travel book, is
among the period's most interesting explorations of
the nature of war, a subject that preoccupied young
writers of the 1930s.

Maturing in the interval between the two world
wars, Isherwood and his contemporaries were
haunted by the memories of the Great War, in
which they were too young to participate, and by
the prospect of a global conflict looming ever more
ominously on the horizon of the future. In *Lions
and Shadows,* he explains that "Like most of my
generation, I was obsessed by a complex of terrors
and longings connected with the idea 'War.' 'War,'
in this purely neurotic sense, meant The Test. The

test of your courage, of your maturity, of your sexual prowess: 'Are you really a Man?' "

All of Isherwood's work of the 1930s is influenced by this obsession with war and with The Test. The Test provides the measure for two of his recurring character types, the Truly Strong Man and the Truly Weak Man. The former has no need to prove himself, while the latter is a neurotic hero, plagued by self-doubt, who seizes every opportunity to test his courage. "The Truly Strong Man," Isherwood observes in *Lions and Shadows*, "travels straight across the broad America of normal life, taking always the direct, reasonable route. But 'America' is just what the truly weak man . . . dreads. And so, with immense daring, with an infinitely greater expenditure of nervous energy, money, time, physical and mental resources, he prefers to attempt the huge northern circuit, the laborious, terrible north-west passage, avoiding life; and his end, if he does not turn back, is to be lost for ever in the blizzard and the ice."

The Truly Weak Man is doomed always to fail or to elude The Test, even when he appears to have succeeded. Since The Test originates in deeply rooted self-doubt, the Truly Weak Man can never be satisfied that he has successfully passed it, and he is impelled forward to ever new tests. Daring and heroic acts thus become indexes of private insecurity. The effect of Isherwood's myth of the neurotic hero is to reinterpret the nature of heroism itself as disguised weakness.

One source of the neurosis that afflicts the Truly Weak Man is his domineering mother, a Freudian carnivore who destroys her child by arresting his maturity. Cyril Connolly describes the Evil Mother as "fierce, obstinate, tearful, and conventional."[1] The Evil Mother and the Truly Weak

Man are locked in mortal combat, and yet their relationship is also one of symbiotic need. The struggle
of mothers and sons is a recurring theme in
Isherwood's work, especially prominent in *All
the Conspirators, The Memorial,* and *The Ascent
of F 6.*

Like the Berlin stories, Isherwood's other
works of the 1930s also integrate private and public
concerns. The two early novels are particularly successful in portraying a society in uneasy transition.
Isherwood's miniaturist technique—his concretely
detailed accounts of individual predicaments—invests his characters with symbolic significance as
social types, and the narrowly focused novels capture the breadth of an entire society. They depict
the frustrations of a rootless generation, adrift in a
world without positive values. The collaborations
with Auden are more obviously political. In fact, the
plays are burdened by the clumsiness of their di-
dacticism. But *Journey to a War* brilliantly explores
the relationship of the public and the private by
documenting war's impact on the inner life.

All the Conspirators

Begun when Isherwood was twenty-one years old
and published in 1928, when he was twenty-three,
All the Conspirators is very much a young man's
novel. "It records," Isherwood later wrote, "a minor
engagement in what Shelley calls 'the great war between the old and young.' "[2] Heavily indebted to E.
M. Forster, and to a lesser extent to James Joyce and
Virginia Woolf, the novel is studiedly avant-garde
in its cinematic montages, stream of consciousness,
abrupt shifts in points of view, coded language and

consequent obscurity. But for all its derivativeness, it is astonishingly assured in its command of technique and tone.

The novel introduces the Evil Mother and the Truly Weak Man, and it reveals Isherwood's mastery of ironic perspective and of the Forsterian tea-tabling method used to such advantage in the Berlin stories. And like the later works, the novel suggests connections between individual predicaments and large social issues. But in addition to providing glimpses of a brilliance more fully realized in subsequent novels, *All the Conspirators* is important in and of itself.

The book focuses on the relationship of the would-be artist Philip Lindsay and his widowed mother. It opens on the Scilly Isles, where Philip, after abruptly quitting his dull office job, has fled with his friend Allen, a medical student and amateur artist. At the hotel, Philip renews his acquaintance with a former schoolmate, Victor Page, to whom he condescends yet attempts to impress. When Allen disgraces him by appearing drunk in public, Philip returns to London to face his mother like an errant schoolboy. After much pressure from her, he shamefacedly agrees to return to his job.

When Victor Page visits the family, he is quickly recognized by Mrs. Lindsay as an excellent match for Philip's sister Joan. After a courtship discreetly stage-managed by Mrs. Lindsay, Victor and Joan become engaged. In response to Philip's complaints about the dullness of his office work, Victor arranges a job offer in Kenya for him. Despite the pleas of Joan and Allen, Philip accepts the position. But the night before he is scheduled to leave for Africa, he flees home and suffers an attack of rheumatic fever.

The novel ends with a coddled Philip being

nursed back to health by Joan, who has become increasingly alienated from Victor. When Philip sells
three paintings at a society art show and wins second prize in a newspaper-sponsored poetry contest,
Mrs. Lindsay acquiesces in his artistic career. In the
final scenes, Joan writes Victor proposing that they
be married immediately, and Philip castigates Allen
for timidity, telling him, "You refuse to venture,
that's what it is."

All the Conspirators devastatingly indicts the
corrosive influence of the family and the inability of
the young to escape the domination of the old. The
book is not impartial in its indictment, since the
failures of the young people can be traced to the
complacency and hypocrisy of the old. But Isherwood's irony embraces young and old alike, and
all the characters are implicated in the conspiracy to perpetuate the conventional values that sus-
tain an exhausted and morally bankrupt society.
This conspiracy stunts the growth of the young people. It arrests their emotional development and
eventually causes Philip to retreat to the helplessness of childhood.

The intergenerational hostility in the novel is
concentrated most fully in the conflict between
Philip and Mrs. Lindsay, the Truly Weak Man and
the Evil Mother. Ironically, however, the two opponents are finally revealed as complementary images
of each other. They employ the same tactics of "domestic guerilla warfare," and both exploit their apparent weakness as sources of strength in their continual battles. Moreover, they are locked together in
mutual need. Neither can accomplish anything
without the other. When Philip is away, Mrs. Lindsay grows morose and takes to bed. When she is absent, Philip casts others, especially Allen and Joan,
in her role. When he whiningly complains to Joan,

for instance, she realizes that "as so often, he was addressing not her but their mother."

The irony of the novel focuses most completely on Philip, who is gradually exposed as fatuous and priggish. He attacks the sterility of middle-class conventionality, but he relishes the comforts of the Kensington household and he icily condemns Allen's drunkenness on the island, reflecting his mother's bourgeois values. Posing as an artist, Philip claims to desire independence from his mother and freedom from the stultifying dullness of his office job. But his desire for independence is as phoney as his artistic pretensions.

Philip's plan to escape to Kenya is a version of The Test that the Truly Weak Man inevitably imposes on himself, a test that he is doomed to fail or to elude. The need for the test reveals his weakness and insecurity. Emigration has no meaning for Philip except in terms of its effect on his mother. As Allen points out, he wants to go to Africa in order to punish his mother, just as a child hopes to be killed by castor oil in order to prove his nurse a murderess. By the end of the novel, Philip does in fact revert to schoolboy dependence. The rheumatic fever, the same disease that helped him avoid prep school, renders him an invalid, who "mustn't be put out or crossed in the least little thing," as Mrs. Lindsay explains.

Mrs. Lindsay is similarly hypocritical. Her feigned helplessness conceals an iron will. She manipulates the lives of everyone in the book, skillfully pitting one character against another. She claims to want to see her son "safely launched" on a career of his own. But what she really desires is to prolong his dependence on her. She encourages his immaturity and caters to his illnesses. When she appears at the end of the novel, after Philip's attack of rheumatic fever, she is triumphant: "She was radiant. She no longer seemed slightly timid, slightly apprehensive of something unpleasant about to happen. She was confidently gay."

Mrs. Lindsay's new confidence results from the unholy accommodation that she and her son have reached. This accommodation allows Philip to escape the responsibilities of a boring office job and to pursue a dilettantish artistic career. For him, the new arrangement represents a retreat from maturity. For Mrs. Lindsay, the arrangement maintains her position of dominance, while assuring her son's continuing dependence on her. In this generational contest, the older generation preserves its power. But the victory is pyrrhic at best, for the frustration and puerility of the young people contain the seeds of social disaster.

All the younger characters participate in the neurotic conspiracy that deprives them of power and responsibility. Victor Page, a Cambridge hearty devoted to fresh air and exercise, appears the least neurotic of young men imaginable. But his uncritical conformity to the values of the older generation actually exacts a heavy price of him, rendering him manipulable by both Mrs. Lindsay and Philip and, more seriously, stunting his capacity for love. His brutal repression of homosexual feelings for a schoolmate leaves him frightened of sex. When Joan kisses him passionately for the first time, he is clumsy and embarrassed: he "was scarlet in the face . . . He looked half asphyxiated." He finds it impossible to verbalize his feelings for Joan, and he thinks of marriage as "like the jolly out-door sort of friendship of a pair of boys."

Joan is the most sympathetic and most clear-sighted character in the novel. But she is paralyzingly passive. She is manipulated by all the other

characters, and she is unable to act on her percep-
tions, to rebel against her mother, to express her dissatisfaction with Victor, or to pursue her attraction
for Allen. Only when Philip becomes ill does Joan
confront her mother, and even then it is likely that
the confrontation has been engineered by Mrs.
Lindsay. Joan devotes herself to Philip, abandoning
her own life in the process. At the end of the novel,
however, she writes to Victor asking that they be
married soon. This may represent a desperate attempt to escape the unhealthy atmosphere of her
home, and she herself regards it as a betrayal of her
family. But her flight into marriage with someone
she does not love is actually one more act of conformity.

Allen comes closest of the characters to being a
normative figure, embodying most positively the
novel's system of values. A medical student, he
understands Philip's neurotic attachment to his mother. He diagnoses Philip by telling him, "your
imagination wants lancing. It's swollen with pus."
But Allen himself suffers an acute case of boredom,
which, he says, "belongs to the group of cancerous
diseases." Moreover, his ironic detachment betrays
his psychic illness. "My callousness is diseased," he
remarks, "I half admired those men who fainted,
last week, when we watched the operation." His
failure to act on his attraction for Joan is the most
serious manifestation of this callousness. Thus, as
Brian Finney notes, when Philip accuses Allen of
refusing to venture into life, "the irony is double-
edged because the accusation is not without truth
even though it is truer of the accuser than of the
accused."[3]

All the Conspirators depicts the frustration of a
whole generation of middle-class young people.
Spared the tests of war and economic deprivation,

they are intimidated by their own fears. Cajoled
into conformity, they are overly protected and emotionally scarred by an older generation devoted to
values increasingly anachronistic in a society irre-
vocably altered by the Great War. Dominated by
the Evil Mother, the family is the social agency
most guilty of maiming the young. But while the
young people are depicted as victims, they are also
exposed as Truly Weak. Although they recognize
the hypocrisy, snobbery, and philistinism of their
elders, they participate in the conspiracy against
their own maturity.

The novel is not uniformly successful. The self-
consciously avant-garde narrative techniques frequently distract, and the characterization and plot
occasionally falter. But the book's sustained irony
often yields unexpected depths of understanding,
and its fierce depiction of the emptiness of conventional values gives it real power. *All the Conspirators* is a serious anatomy of middle-class malaise, a
remarkably accomplished work for so young an author.

The Memorial

Isherwood's second novel, *The Memorial: Portrait
of a Family,* published in 1932 by the Hogarth
Press, is a more ambitious book than *All the Conspirators* and more completely successful. Like its
predecessor, *The Memorial* depicts the frustration
of English middle-class life in the 1920s, features
versions of the Evil Mother and the Truly Weak
Man, and explores the continuing impact of the past
on the present. But its tone is less angry than that of
the first novel and its vision more mature.

The subject of the book is the continuing ef-

fects of the Great War on English society, and it ex-
amines these effects through a complex portrait of a
single family. In *Lions and Shadows,* Isherwood
describes *The Memorial* as "an epic disguised as a
drawing-room comedy," and he explains his intention to avoid continuous narrative in favor of loosely
connected, self-contained scenes. The novel is thus
"an album of snapshots," dating from different periods, juxtaposed in an apparently haphazard manner. A measure of the novel's success is that these
snapshots finally do yield a portrait of epic scope: "a
genuine interpretation of the times," as Frank Kermode describes the book.[4]

The novel is divided into four parts. The first
part, set in 1928, introduces the surviving members
of the squirearchical Vernon family, now dispersed
from their ancestral home: Mary Scriven, the rebellious Vernon daughter who shocked her family by
an imprudent marriage, and her children, Anne and
Maurice; Lily Vernon, the still-grieving widow of
Richard, the Vernon heir-apparent killed in the war;
their diffident son Eric, now immersed in social
causes; and Richard's homosexual friend, Edward
Blake, a war hero who unsuccessfully attempts suicide in Berlin.

The second section is set in 1920, and the characters introduced in the first section reappear as
they were then. The central event of the section,
and of the novel as a whole, is the dedication of a
war memorial at which all the major characters appear, including the old squire John Vernon, help-
lessly senile and fussed over by family retainers,
and Ramsbotham, a newly rich manufacturer who
will later purchase the Vernon home.

In the third section, the time is 1925. Eric and
Maurice are at Cambridge, the former a troubled intellectual, the latter a charming but irresponsible

hearty. The major action of the section centers
around Edward Blake's visit to Maurice and Eric's
jealous accusation that Blake exercises an unhealthy influence over his cousin.

The final part of the novel is set in 1929.
Maurice, Edward, and Mary accompany Anne and
her fiancé, Tommy Ramsbotham, on an impromptu
visit to the Hall, now in disrepair, owned by the
Ramsbothams and devoid of meaning for the
Vernons. Lily, still devoted to the past, continues
her role as war widow, ably supported by her wor-
shipful admirer Major Charlesworth. Eric converts
to Roman Catholicism. Edward, after fleeing a sex-
less relationship with his artist friend Margaret, returns to Berlin. There, his young homosexual lover,
who can barely remember the war, remarks, "that
War . . . it ought never to have happened."

Isherwood gathers together three generations
of the Vernon family at the dedication of the Chapel
Bridge War Memorial. His account of the dedication is among his most accomplished writing. He
skillfully cuts from the interior monologue of one
character to the thoughts of another and laces the
whole with the empty platitudes of the officiating
bishop, stunningly revealing the complexity of motives hidden behind the masks of official grief and
hollow sentiment. The bishop announces, "To-day
we are gathered together at the foot of this Cross by
a common sorrow and with a common purpose." But
the reactions of the characters actually have very little in common. They are divided even in their
shared loss.

Carefully costumed for a grief only half genuine, motivated as much by self-pity as by love for
Richard, Lily Vernon winces at the alphabetical
reading of the names of the fallen. "Why couldn't
they have read out the officers' names first?" she

asks, and regrets that "There was a great deal of Socialism in the village ... since the War." She pushes forward the senile squire John Vernon to lay the first wreath on the monument, sealing his position as chief mourner. The living symbol of a passing era, the old man is too feeble to feel anything. As Mary observes, "Landowners were becoming obsolete. Father was obsolete." For him, the war actually meant little: he "could still, even when they were shelling Paris, take his drives."

For Mary, herself a war widow, though an unacknowledged one, the war "meant filling in ration-cards, visiting the Hospital, getting up jumble sales for the Red Cross." She denounces the "cult of dead people" as snobbery and describes the memorial service as "not only false but ... actually wicked. Living people are better than dead ones." To Edward Blake, the most genuine mourner, the war means only that "Richard is dead. And this is what remains ... the doll in her black, the slobbering old man, the gawky boy getting into the carriage." For Eric, the gawky boy, the memorial signifies the war's continuing legacy of guilt and self-doubt. In ways the characters themselves only dimly sense, they are all casualties of the war.

The book's shifting time scheme, beginning in 1928, moving backward to the pivotal event of 1920, then forward to 1925, and finally culminating in a 1929 postscript, might be expected to underline the inevitable changes wrought by time. Yet the effect is precisely opposite. The shifting time scheme actually emphasizes the static quality of the internal lives of the characters, all of whom remain imprisoned in the past. Even those characters who most frenetically attempt to escape the past or to alter the present are paralyzed by the effects of the momentous event antecedent to the novel, the Great War.

Externally, much change does take place. The old squire and his wife die, the Hall decays and passes into the ownership of nouveaux riches tradesmen, children mature, residences are relocated, relationships begin and dissolve. The novel, in fact, traces the dissolution of a representative, tradition-bound gentry family, and in the process documents some of the fundamental alterations in English society initiated by the war. That the Vernon family is representative of an entire class rendered increasingly anachronistic in the 1920s gives the characters symbolic significance and the novel broad scope.[5]

But, typically, Isherwood's emblematic method proceeds by immersion in the particular; and the social history that his novel encapsulates serves as a backdrop to its more insistent preoccupation with the interior lives of survivors. The novel's self-conscious shifting of the time frame creates a paradoxical sense of simultaneous flux and stasis: in the midst of enormous social change, the emotional lives of the characters remain arrested in the past.

Isherwood's narrative technique works in concert with the nonconsecutive time scheme to create a complex ambiguity at the heart of the novel. In each section, he presents a series of self-contained scenes, each narrated from the point of view of a different character and developed primarily through interior monologue and flashback. The reader is thus constantly forced to reevaluate the characters and events in light of new perspectives introduced by changing points of view, as the initial impression of one character is qualified by the perception of another or by a snapshot from a different time and place. No character can be trusted to understand fully either himself or the other characters. The shifts in time and in points of view emphasize the subjectivity of experience and the relativity of truth.

The Forsterian tea-tabling technique also contributes to the ambiguity of the novel. Crucial information is reported matter-of-factly or buried in a welter of apparently insignificant details. For instance, Mary's clandestine courtship by an improvident but charming Irishman is almost totally subordinated to the conventional engagement of Lily and Richard; Eric's pivotal decision to sell the Hall takes place entirely off-stage; Maurice's involvement in a foolhardy auto accident that kills one of his Cambridge classmates is revealed without comment; and Anne's relationship with Tommy Ramsbotham is deliberately underplayed. By understating or avoiding potentially large or melodramatic scenes, Isherwood brilliantly exploits the power of reticence. Despite an almost overwhelming abundance of circumstantial detail, situations and characters remain mysterious and fascinating. They resist neat explanations and continually invite speculation.

The ambiguity of *The Memorial* is born not of indecision or lack of clarity but of maturity. It results from Isherwood's fully developed understanding of the complexity of life at a time of rapid social change and of the difficulty in judging others. As a consequence, there are no villains in *The Memorial*. Nor are any of the characters idealized. Each is flawed, and some a great deal more than others. But Isherwood portrays them all as victims of forces over which they have little personal control.

Isherwood's easy identification with all of his characters as the narrative moves from one point of view to another signals an empathetic response to them quite absent in his depiction of the characters in *All the Conspirators,* a work narrated from the point of view of the young people and one that frequently condescends to rather than identifies with its characters. The new empathy of *The Memorial* dissipates the anger that dominates the earlier novel, even as the later book recreates versions of the Evil Mother and the Truly Weak Man, those figures so fiercely indicted in *All the Conspirators. The Memorial* is thus informed by the compassionate understanding that is a hallmark of Isherwood's later work.

The discontinuous narrative of the second novel also contributes to the sense of fragmentation that pervades the book. Although the characters are linked by ties of family and friendship, they are nevertheless isolated from each other. They frequently attempt to break down the walls of isolation, to reach out to their fellows. But these attempts all fail, for the characters are unable to communicate meaningfully and they persistently misinterpret each other. They all suffer the effects of war, but the war has affected each of them differently. Unable to share their experience with others, they remain isolated in the prisons of the self.

The character most literally isolated is Lily, the war widow dedicated to the cult of the past, to the "old safe, happy, beautiful world" destroyed by the war and by subsequent social change. Alienated from her son, she lives alone in a London apartment, her sole activity membership in a society that visits historical sites, her only relationship a coquettish, nonintimate flirtation with Maj. Charlesworth, a fellow reactionary romantic. At the death of her husband, Lily retired from life, convinced that "nothing can possibly happen which will touch me again," a prophecy that proves self-fulfilling. Ten years after her bereavement, she still

dresses exclusively in black. She deliberately cultivates an air of sadness, but as Eric observes, "she
doesn't feel." Her only sign of vitality is the "extraordinary passion of quiet resentment" with
which she challenges the future and laments the
loss of the past.

Like Mrs. Lindsay, Lily is a version of the Evil
Mother. She feigns weakness as a means of
strength, and she is especially adept at inducing
guilt. When Eric accuses her of lacking feeling, for
instance, he immediately contradicts himself: "No,
he thought, that's utterly unjust. I'm a brute. I'm
vile to her." Her snobbery, pretentiousness, conventionality, and absurdly romantic misinterpreta-
tions of history all make her unattractive. Yet she is
by no means simply the manipulative, stifling
mother that Mrs. Lindsay is. Her bewilderment at
the passing of the Edwardian age makes her touch-
ingly vulnerable; and her admission, "I often wonder . . . how much of my interest in the Past is genuine," may indicate a degree of self-knowledge.
Moreover, her charge that those who would wan-
tonly destroy the past have nothing to put in its
place is not without substance.

The other characters of *The Memorial* explore a
number of alternatives to the worship of the past.
They attempt to give meaning to their lives by variously embracing social and cultural activities, daredevil adventures, social and political causes, religion, and sex. Yet they remain inwardly empty and
emotionally needy, more victims of the past than
participants in the present. None of their feverish
activity fully satisfies, and the novel breathes an air
of futility.

Mary Scriven is the most attractive character in
the book, and as a rebel against the old order and a
champion of the new, she serves as a foil to Lily. But
she is not the ideal character some critics assume.
As Paul Piazza remarks, "Lily denies life; Mary im-

personates it."[6] She crowds her life with parties and games, yet she remains empty within. She attempts to convince herself that "she had done with the Past." But despite her declaration that "the Past couldn't hurt her now," it nevertheless continues to intrude on her present.

Mary's unhappy marriage leaves her despising men and as incapable of genuine feeling as Lily. In compensation, she cultivates a sense of detachment that distances her from meaningful relationships with others, and she cloaks her personal disappointment in self-deprecating humor. Anne echoes Eric's charge against Lily when she asks, regarding Mary, "Had she ever really felt anything at all?" Famous for her party impersonations of Queen Victoria, Mary, on her final appearance in the novel, agrees to a "very, very last performance," to which Maurice shouts, "Liar!" The epithet is appropriate, for Mary is doomed to mask her unhappiness in charades.

Eric attempts to assuage his unhappiness by involvement first in left-wing political causes and finally in religion. But he is the Truly Weak Man, and his faddish allegiances—calculated reactions against his conventional mother—are functions of his neurosis rather than of real commitment. Feeling an irrational guilt over not having fought in the war that killed his father, he is haunted by self-doubt and by an obsessive love-hate relationship with his mother.

Betrayed by Lily's retreat into the past, Eric attempts constantly to shock her into feeling. But his cultivated image of social concern disguises his own failure of feeling. Secretly in love with Maurice, he represses his homosexuality. He pressures Edward to break off his liaison with Maurice only to admit to himself, "I was jealous. The whole thing was nothing but jealousy." His flight to the Roman Catholic Church at the end of the novel is

analogous to Philip Lindsay's reversion to childhood in *All the Conspirators*, a retreat into the arms
of maternal authority.

The novel's most memorable character, Edward Blake, is another version of the Truly Weak
Man. His insecurity is measured by his constant
need to test himself: "He dared refuse no adventure—horribly frightened as he often was. He
would have fought any boy in the school, would
have got himself expelled for any offence, rather
than admit to being afraid." His attraction for Richard is an attraction of apparent opposites. He
casts Richard as the Truly Strong Man, one who
"had no need to give proofs of his courage, to assert
the strength of his will." But Richard fails him, and
Edward interprets his friend's marriage to Lily and
his rejection of Mary—"Richard's single act of cowardice"—as personal betrayals. Edward has traveled around the world, "shot big game, climbed in
the Alps, been round the coasts of Europe in a small
sailing boat," and recklessly made himself a flying
ace in the war he did not expect to survive. But he
has never been able to escape the impact of
Richard's loss.

Edward's rejection of life is clear from his bun-
gled suicide attempt, presented early in the novel.
But that denial is implicit as well in his restless
search for excitement as a daredevil test pilot and in
his frustrating inability to combine love and sex.
The slyly manipulative and maternal Margaret is in
love with him, but he is not sexually attracted to
her; and he is unable to establish a stable homosexual union. Margaret's confidence in their relationship—"Somehow I feel awfully secure. About us
two, I mean"—is misplaced. Ironically, her faith
that sex will become less important to Edward is
expressed in a letter that he reads while awaiting

the arrival of his German boyfriend Franz. The emptiness of Edward's life—and of the lives of all the novel's war casualties—is perfectly captured in Franz's solemnly conventional sentiment, "that War . . . it ought never to have happened."

The banality of Franz's remark both mocks the genuine suffering of Isherwood's characters and poignantly underlines it. They are adrift in a world without purpose. They recognize the hollow ring of old platitudes, but they have discovered no new source of meaning. The future promises to be as bleak as the present. Anne's forthcoming marriage to the inhibited Ramsbotham heir is a marriage of convenience, yet another failure of feeling, one fittingly commemorated by Lily's gift of Jacobean silver, a gesture as futile as the marriage itself. But in *The Memorial*, failures of feeling are the inevitable consequence of the all-encompassing failure represented by the war. The novel offers no positive alternatives, and its bleak vision is relieved only by the compassionate acceptance of its empathetic author.

The Memorial is an impressive achievement. Like *All the Conspirators*, it depicts the middle-class malaise of the 1920s, but it does so with new compassion and understanding, with a breadth of vision born of maturity. Isherwood's mastery of narrative technique and his brilliant manipulation of the time scheme give his "album of snapshots" extraordinary depth and scope. The characters are depicted with remarkable clarity of detail, and the concrete particularity in which they are rendered helps make them symbolic of an entire society, adrift and uncertain. This "epic disguised as a drawing-room comedy" sings the hidden costs of the Great War in a chorus of the walking wounded.

Collaborations with Auden

Isherwood's collaborations with W. H. Auden in writing three experimental verse dramas and a remarkable travel book earned him the reputation of ideological commitment in an intensely political decade. But the artistic union of the decade's finest poet and its most sensitive prose stylist did not produce great literature, at least in part because of the overtly political stance the collaborators assumed. They so heavy-handedly imposed political dogma upon the plays that dramatic development and thematic coherence suffered.

With the exception of *Journey to a War*, the Auden-Isherwood collaboration yielded work less satisfying than that produced by either writer separately. As Stephen Spender observes, "most of the poetry in these plays is inferior to the poetry of Auden's single poems; no character in them has the subtlety and profundity of characters in Mr. Isherwood's novels."[7]

The plays, written for Rupert Doone's Group Theatre, are frankly experimental reactions against traditional dramatic realism.[8] They incorporate elements of the political cabaret, German expressionism, the fairy tale, and the pantomime, while deliberately eschewing subtlety in both characterization and theme. Auden declared that "the development of the film has deprived drama of any excuse for being documentary . . . . The subject of drama . . . is the commonly known, the universally familiar stories of the society or generation in which it is written . . . . the drama is not suited to the analysis of character, which is the province of the novel. Dramatic characters are simplified, easily recognisable and over life-size."[9] However serious as an attempt to make a moribund theater relevant as a forum for the exploration of contemporary issues, Auden's concept of the new drama actually rendered superfluous his collaborator's special talents for ironic observation and for shrewd insight into individual motivation.

The Dog Beneath the Skin, or Where is Francis?, produced in 1936, is an exuberant satire of contemporaneous political confusion. It is frequently very funny, but it lacks a sure sense of direction and, as a consequence, its effects are often adolescent. The episodic plot traces the mythic quest of Alan Norman in his search for a missing heir, Sir Francis Crewe. Accompanied by a dog, Alan travels through Europe, visiting a reactionary monarchy and a lunatic fascist state. He returns to England, where he finds fascism in his native village and discovers that the object of his quest has been with him all along, disguised as the dog Francis.

After a general denunciation—"most of you will die without ever knowing what your leaders are really fighting for or even that you are fighting at all"—Alan, Francis, and a handful of villagers depart to become "a unit in the army of the other side." Unfortunately, the "other side" is so imprecisely identified as to convict the play of superficiality in its political analysis.

The Ascent of F 6, published in 1936 but not produced until 1937, is an altogether more serious poetic drama. It moves beyond topical satire to explore the nature of the will to power. The play's external plot is organized around the international competition to scale a politically significant mountain straddling the border of two colonies, British Sudoland and Ostnian Sudoland. In developing this plot, the play exposes the corruption of politics and the emptiness of contemporary daily life, the latter creating the public's voracious appetite for heroes.

After much reluctance, Michael Ransom agrees to lead the British climbing expedition, and the journey up the mountain is paralleled by Ransom's interior journey of self-discovery.

Ransom, whose name suggests his sacrificial role, is modeled on T. E. Lawrence, whom Isherwood described in 1937 as having "suffered, in his own person, the neurotic ills of an entire generation."[10] Ransom's decision to undertake the climb is motivated not by the jingoistic appeals of his brother, the prime minister, but by his attachment to his mother. A reincarnation of the Evil Mother, Mrs. Ransom is finally exposed as her son's personal Demon. After losing all the members of his climbing party, Ransom reaches the summit of F 6, where, in an expressionistic delirium, he confronts the phantoms of his guilt. The hallucination culminates in the appearance of his mother as a young woman. He dies with his head buried in her lap.

The most fully developed character in the Auden-Isherwood plays, Michael Ransom is an intriguing study in heroism. His mother tells him, "you were to be the truly strong." But on his quest he exposes himself as one more version of the Truly Weak Man. He discovers that he is as flawed in his personal life as, more obviously, his brother is in his public life. Ransom is corrupted both by allowing himself to be used for imperialistic interests and by sacrificing others in the course of his personal quest for power.

The play is brilliantly unified by patterns of linguistic and structural echoes, but its discovery of the will to power in an Oedipal source is both annoyingly simplistic and unconvincingly realized. *The Ascent of F 6* is, in fact, a deeply flawed play, confused as well as confusing. But for all its obvious faults, the work remains fascinating in its haunting exploration of the will to power; and its recreation of the Evil Mother and the Truly Weak Man link it firmly to the Isherwood canon.

The final play of the Auden-Isherwood collaboration, *On the Frontier*, is less experimental and more unified than its two predecessors. Produced in 1938, the play's obsession with war has an immediacy that partially compensates for the crudity of its characterization and the predictability of its politics. Creating two mythic states, the monarchist Ostnia and the fascist Westland, the play savagely indicts nationalism and looks forward to a future city where "the will of love is done." The plot traces the movement of the two countries toward a war that channels the energies of workers away from the class struggle and into a self-defeating xenophobia.

The effect of the war is imaginatively portrayed by the simultaneous reactions of two families on the stage, one occupying the Ostnian side of the frontier, the other the Westland side, each oblivious of the other. The Westland son and the Ostnian daughter love each other, but they are unable to cross the artificial boundaries of hysteria and hatred erected by nationalism. They embrace only after death in an embarrassingly sentimental *Liebestod*.

On the Frontier is subtitled "a melodrama." The term fairly acknowledges the play's exaggerated emotion, stock characterization, and comic-strip simplicity. All the characters are stereotypes, including the fascist Leader, who is yet another Truly Weak Man. Much the most intriguing character, because more subtly drawn and more fully human, is Valerian, the power-hungry capitalist. Unfortunately, the two lovers are the most insipid of characters. Since they carry the burden of the play's version of a better world, the Just City comes dangerously close to the platitudinous. Although it lacks the zany fun of *The Dog Beneath the Skin* and the poetic complexity of *The Ascent of F 6, On the Frontier* successfully depicts the dangers of nationalism and of propaganda; and it effectively portrays the metaphorical boundaries that separate countries, classes, and individuals.

Journey to a War is the only really distinguished product of the Auden-Isherwood collaboration, and its success may result from a strict division of labor, one that allowed each partner to exploit his individual strengths. The book resulted from a commission by two publishing houses, Random House of New York and Faber & Faber of London, to write a travel book about the East. The collaborators decided to go to China and report on the Sino-Japanese War. They left London in January 1938 and returned at the end of July. The book appeared in 1939 and consists of four separate but related parts: prefatory sonnets by Auden, a "Travel-Diary" written by Isherwood and based on journals kept by both travelers, a group of photographs taken by Auden, and "In Time of War," a sonnet sequence with verse commentary by Auden.

The "Travel-Diary" is by far the longest section of the book. Its particularity complements the universality of Auden's poetry: it documents the specific journey and the reactions of the two individual travelers in concrete detail, while Auden's poems take as their subject the generalized question of war in the abstract. Significantly, both men abandon the ideological rhetoric that burdens the plays. They are clearly committed to the Chinese cause, but their political point of view is the liberal humanism saluted in Auden's dedicatory sonnet, "To E. M. Forster": "You promise still the inner life shall pay." Like Forster, Auden and Isherwood calculate the cost of war in terms of its destructiveness to the human spirit; but the younger men also endorse their mentor's faith, expressed in *Howards End,* that "There are moments when the inner life actually 'pays,' when years of self-scrutiny, conducted for no ulterior motive, are suddenly of practical use."[11]

The personal response to war, its impact on the inner life, is indeed the prevailing theme of the book. Isherwood's wonderful description of a Japanese air raid weaves into the apparently objective reporting a personal response that colors the whole:

The searchlights criss-crossed, plotting points, like dividers; and suddenly there they were, six of them, flying close together and high up. It was as if a microscope had brought dramatically into focus the bacilli of a fatal disease. They passed, bright, tiny, and deadly, infecting the night. . . . It was as tremendous as Beethoven, but *wrong*—a cosmic offence, and an insult to the whole of Nature and the entire earth. I don't know if I was frightened. Something inside me was flapping about like a fish.

The personal element is also emphasized by the concurrent development of an emerging portrait of Auden as the Truly Strong Man, the foil to Isherwood's self-portrait as a Truly Weak Man. The contrast is apparent in the following passage: "I slept uneasily that night—in my trousers and shirt: not wishing to have to leave the train and bolt for cover in my pajamas. Auden, with his monumental calm, had completely undressed."

The "Travel-Diary" is studiedly antiheroic in its presentation of war. With characteristic understatement and ironic humor, Isherwood continually explores the nature of war. He searches for a definition that will embrace war's absurdity, stupidity, pettiness, and monotony as well as its suffering and waste:

War is bombing an already disused arsenal, missing it, and killing a few old women. War is lying in a stable with a gangrenous leg. War is drinking hot water in a barn and worrying about one's wife. War is a handful of lost and terrified men in the mountains, shooting at something moving in the undergrowth. War is waiting for days with nothing to do; shouting down a dead telephone; going without sleep, or sex, or a wash. War is untidy, inefficient, obscure, and largely a matter of chance.

The strength of the diary is that it creates from the narrow experience of two naive young men—limited by their own ignorance and fears and dependent on translators and bureaucrats—a vivid account of the human realities of war.

The 1930s was the decade of Isherwood's greatest productivity and of his emergence as a genuine hope of English fiction. The early novels and the Auden-Isherwood collaborations were for a long time eclipsed by the popularity of the Berlin stories. The neglect of *The Memorial* was particularly unfortunate, for that work brilliantly dissects the hopelessness of an entire society by empathetically conveying the personal loneliness and private neuroses of a handful of memorable characters. The acuity of its insight and the mastery of its execution earn that early novel an honored position in the Isherwood canon. But the collaborative works and *All the Conspirators* also deserve the new attention that they have recently received. Taken together, they articulate the frustrations and obsessions of a tormented decade dominated by Evil Mothers and Truly Weak Men.

4

~~~~~~

The Pain of Hunger
Beneath Everything:
Prater Violet

Although set in London in the 1930s, *Prater Violet*
is the first novel that Isherwood wrote in America.
Published in 1945, first in *Harper's Bazaar* and
then separately, it features a naive narrator who
bears the author's own name and a delightful major
character who is reminiscent of Mr. Norris. *Prater
Violet* at first glance appears to be a continuation of
the Berlin stories in a different place and in a lighter
vein. But the lightness of the novel is a charming
illusion: *Prater Violet*'s brilliant surface conceals
beneath its comic veneer a depth of seriousness
equal to that of *Goodbye to Berlin*.

Within its brief compass, *Prater Violet* explores
themes as diverse and as weighty as the role of the
artist in modern society, the search for a father, the
problem of identity, and finally, the quest for transcendence. Unobtrusively informed by its author's
newly discovered faith in Vedantism, *Prater Violet*
is ultimately a religious novel. For all its obvious
similarities to the earlier works, the book signals a
departure for Isherwood and a new beginning.

The slight plot revolves around the developing
relationship between the narrator and Friedrich
Bergmann, a Viennese film director imported to
London by Imperial Bulldog Pictures. Hired to as-
sist Bergmann in writing a script for a film the Aus-

trian is to direct for the company, Christopher is immediately fascinated by the expansive foreigner. The two quickly develop a close personal and professional friendship.

They work together on a stickily sentimental musical comedy about the romance of a poor Viennese flower-girl and the disguised Prince of Borodania. Counterpointing the escapist fatuity of the film is the real plight of Austria and the rise of fascism throughout Europe. The brutal repression of the socialist uprising in Austria fills the newspaper headlines and endangers Bergmann's family in Vienna.

Despite Bergmann's preoccupations with the Austrian political crisis and the minor intrigues at Imperial Bulldog, the movie is finally finished. After a party to celebrate its completion, Bergmann and Christopher walk out together into the London night, fellow travelers on the journey through life, content in each other's company. "He was my father. I was his son," the narrator remarks, "And I loved him very much." The film proves a commercial success, and Bergmann accepts a job offer in Hollywood.

The structure of *Prater Violet* emphasizes the novel's insistent concern with the role of the artist and with the personal relationship of Christopher and Bergmann. In the first part of the book, the two are closeted together in Bergmann's flat, and their discussions of art are as theoretical as they are practical. The second part is set in Imperial Bulldog's cavernous film studio. This second section demonstrates Bergmann's practical mastery of his craft under personal strain and appalling conditions. The final part, occuring after the film's completion, is the most personal and lyrical. Christopher acknowledges Bergmann as his father figure and poses fundamental questions about the meaning of life, presaging his own emergence into maturity.

The personal relationship of the young novelist and the old master is at the heart of the book, unifying all its disparate threads. On their first contact, the two share a sense of déjà vu. "There are meetings which are like recognitions," Christopher reflects, "this was one of them. . . . I knew that face. It was the face of a political situation, an epoch. The face of Central Europe." Bergmann tells him, "I feel absolutely no shame before you. We are like two married men who meet in a whorehouse."

Variously described as an emperor, a tragicomic clown, a "Jewish Socrates," Bergmann thoroughly dominates the "innocent" Christopher, promising him, "I shall proceed to corrupt you. I shall teach you everything from the very beginning." With characteristic exaggeration, the Austrian describes life as a Dantesque journey through hell, casting himself as Dante and Christopher as "the good Virgil who has come to guide me through this Anglo-Saxon comedy." But whereas Virgil's function in the *Divine Comedy* is to lead Dante through the underworld, when Bergmann and Christopher venture into London, the former "was always the guide, and I the tourist."

The exiled Bergmann, a "perpetual stranger" who knows firsthand the horrors of fascism, is Christopher's Virgilian guide into a new awareness of English life and of himself. The director's description of fascism as a spreading plague and his angry denunciation of English insularity are both confirmed by the Austrian crisis and the English reaction to it. This reaction is illustrated most vividly in an egregious journalist's explanation that "it isn't our affair. I mean, you can't expect people in England to care." But it is apparent as well in the profit-centered insensitivity of the film studio executive Chatsworth and, more complexly, in Christopher's own self-doubts.

Politically aware, yet not fully committed, Christopher is yet another Truly Weak Man, trapped in his insecurities. Diagnosed by Bergmann as a "typical mother's son," he exemplifies the dilemma of the would-be revolutionary writer: "He is unable to cut himself free, sternly, from the bourgeois dream of the Mother, that fatal and comforting dream. He wants to crawl back into the economic safety of the womb. He hates the paternal, revolutionary tradition, which reminds him of his duty as a son." Early in his work on the screenplay, Christopher finds himself unable to write acceptable dialogue and attributes the difficulty to the limitations of his class: "I didn't know because, for all my parlor socialism, I was a snob. I didn't know how anybody spoke, except public-school boys and neurotic bohemians."

Bergmann's fertile creativity and genuine anguish contrast with Christopher's artistic paralysis and vague dread. For Christopher, the prospect of war "was as unreal . . . as death itself." A declassed intellectual, he knows what he is supposed to feel, but he actually cares less than he tries to imagine that he does. Conversely, Bergmann feels war as the tangible suffering of "plain human men and women," and he finds art and politics inseparable. He even translates the insipid film he is assigned to direct into a political parable.

But Bergmann is painfully aware of the contrast between the romantic plot of the frivolous motion picture set in Vienna and the real suffering of the city. At one point, he exclaims, "I s--- upon the picture! This heartless filth! This wretched, lying cha-

rade! To make such a picture at such a moment is
definitely heartless. It is a crime." Nevertheless, he
does care about the film, and he allows Chatsworth
to manipulate him into completing it. The success
of the picture vindicates the cynical film editor
Lawrence Dwight's view of art as a means of fighting anarchy, "Reclaiming life from its natural mud-
dle. Making patterns."

Prater Violet thus documents the limits of the
artist in contemporary society.[1] Chatsworth, a deli-
cious caricature of the vulgar businessman, actually
dictates to Bergmann a denouement for the film,
and the incipient fascism of the movie industry is
underlined by Bergmann's equation of the studio's
executives with Germany's Nazis, who are concurrently conducting the Reichstag fire trial. But
Bergmann's inspired direction represents the triumph of the creative artist even under wretched
conditions. The defeat of anarchy is due not to
Dwight's ideal of technical perfection but to
Bergmann's personal artistry: "His absolute cer-
tainty swept us along like a torrent. There were
hardly any retakes. The necessary script alterations
seemed to write themselves. Bergmann knew exactly what he wanted."

Bergmann's devotion to his work may be seen
as an illustration of the Vedantist doctrine of "nonattached action, of work performed as ritual, which
the *Bhagavad-Gita* teaches."[2] According to this belief, all work becomes important in and of itself,
without regard for its immediate consequences: "It
is only toward the results of work that [the doer of
nonattached action] remains indifferent . . . . This,
in its development, is the attitude of a saint. When
action is done in this spirit, Krishna teaches, it will
lead us to true wisdom, to the knowledge of what is
behind action, behind all life: the ultimate reality."[3]

Thus, despite his own belief that art and politics are inseparable, Bergmann's inspired work on a reactionary film may actually advance his spiritual growth. The first of Isherwood's secular saints, Bergmann is also the most successfully realized.

Early in the novel, Bergmann and Christopher are described as fellow prisoners; at the end, they are referred to as fellow travelers. The difference in the two epithets is a measure of Christopher's growth in the course of the book, his arrival at a maturity indebted to Bergmann's influence but finally independent of him. That growth is most obvious in the novel's penultimate scene, a beautiful passage of poetic intensity that unfolds Christopher's inner life and casts the book in new perspective.

As Christopher and Bergmann walk out together into a deserted London street lit by lamps of "an unnatural remote brilliance," Christopher observes that "it was that hour of the night at which man's ego almost sleeps." The time is propitious for confronting ultimate questions. He defines himself as "a traveler, a wanderer," and he asks "the only question worth asking our fellow-travelers. What makes you go on living? Why don't you kill yourself? Why is all this bearable? What makes you bear it?" These questions—later formulated as "Who are you? Who am I? What are we doing here?"—are religious questions, and they have haunted the book, surfacing repeatedly in various guises.

Earlier, the film's sound engineer, Roger, remarks, "Sometimes I wonder what all this is for. Why not just peacefully end it?" He explains that the best things in his life have been "good, unexpected lays." But for Christopher, love has been a succession of brief relationships, in which he and his alphabetized lovers are doomed eventually to become "trophies, hung up in the museums of each

other's vanity." The impetus to love has been "the
pain of hunger beneath everything" and the goal of
lovemaking "the dreamless sleep after the orgasm,
which is like death."

In his meditation on death, "the desired, the
feared," Christopher discovers sitting enthroned in
his own heart the arch-fear, "the fear of being
afraid." This discovery of the ego as the source of
the Truly Weak Man's neurosis marks a critical
stage in Christopher's emergent maturity. Indeed,
in a passage that echoes both the Bhagavad Gita and
the *Divine Comedy*,[4] Christopher glimpses beyond
the neurosis to its cure in the Vedantic renunciation
of the self: "And, at this moment, but how infinitely
faint, how distant, like the high far glimpse of a goat
track through the mountains between clouds, I see
something else: the way that leads to safety. To
where there is no fear, no loneliness, no need of J.,
K., L., or M. For a second I glimpse it. For an in-
stant, it is even quite clear."

But Christopher is not yet ready to renounce
his ego: "The clouds shut down, and a breath off the
glacier, icy with the inhuman coldness of the peaks,
touches my cheek. 'No,' I think, 'I could never do it.
Rather the fear I know, the loneliness I know. For
to take that other way would mean that I should lose
myself. I should no longer be Christopher Isherwood.' "

The mystical moment passes. The "way that
leads to safety" is rejected, at least for the present.
But Christopher does not retreat into the pose of the
Truly Weak Man. "Beneath outer consciousness,"
he and Bergmann, "two other beings, anonymous,
impersonal, without labels, had met and recognized
each other, and had clasped hands. He was my father. I was his son. And I loved him very much." In
this simple, extraordinarily tender recognition, two

of the novel's persistent themes—the problem of identity and the search for a father—are beautifully resolved. Christopher joins the fathers after all, thus fulfilling Bergmann's early promise in regard to his mother fixation: "But do not worry. We shall change all that."

Despite Christopher's refusal to embrace Vedantic selflessness, he has progressed along the path of spiritual illumination. Moreover, his recognition of the "pain of hunger beneath everything" may propel him still further along the path. In an important essay published soon after *Prater Violet*, Isherwood describes the posing of fundamental religious questions as "a germ of doubt" that may lead to salvation. Christopher's hunger may reflect his "dissatisfaction with surface consciousness, his need to look more deeply into the meaning of life."[5] The concept is similar to that articulated by Virgil in the *Divine Comedy*, when he urges Dante toward the ascent into Paradise:

> That apple whose sweetness in their craving keen
> Mortals go seeking on so many boughs
> This day shall peace to all thy hungers mean.[6]

In any case, the tentativeness of Christopher's glimpses of spiritual enlightenment is artistically sound, for a sudden religious conversion would lack credibility.

Prater Violet is among the most accomplished short novels in the language. A masterpiece of artistic control, it is that marvelous rarity: a book that is both meaningful and charming. In Diana Trilling's words, "It is gay, witty, sophisticated, but wholly responsible."[7] At once a comic satire of the film industry and a serious study of the relationship of art and life, *Prater Violet* presents both a memorable portrait of a lovable, fully human genius and a chronicle of the journey from neurosis toward transcendence. As Brian Finney comments, "What is so extraordinary about this short and apparently inconsequential novelette is the manner in which Isherwood has fused naturalistic depictions of character and dialogue with a density of texture and meaning that one would normally expect to have made it too ponderous, too burdened with significance. Yet it retains its light touch flawlessly from start to finish."[8] A technical *tour de force, Prater Violet* is also a novel of affirmation.

As the first of Isherwood's novels to be written after his conversion to Vedantism, *Prater Violet* marks a new beginning. The later novels are all informed by an awareness of the "pain of hunger beneath everything." This awareness often expresses a distinction between the *Maya,* or mundane reality, and the *Brahman,* or higher reality; it frequently culminates in a struggle between the "apparent, outer self and an invisible, inner self,"[9] between the ego of individual identity and the *Atman* of universal consciousness, the impersonal God within each individual. The Vedantic influence helps create what Alan Wilde describes as Isherwood's "double vision of man seen through his own eyes and, as it were, through those of God."[10] As in *Prater Violet,* the Vedantic influence tends to be subtle and unobtrusive, enriching but not burdening the novels. As always, Isherwood continues to concern himself with human experience and with the personal plights of individual human beings in an imperfect world.

5

They That Love Beyond the World: *The World in the Evening*

The World in the Evening may be Isherwood's most problematic novel. Upon its publication in 1954, it achieved a wide popular audience, but a generally negative critical response. Its initial popularity may be attributable to the depiction of glamorous and quaint characters in exotic settings, the mildly titillating sex scenes, and the happy ending. In a letter written to his friend Edward Upward soon before the book's publication, Isherwood himself described the novel as "terribly slipshod, and vulgar and sentimental at times in a Hollywoodish way."[1]

But Isherwood's description is far too harsh. The book is not at all slipshod in construction and only occasionally flirts with vulgarity and sentimentality. The novel does contain some unaccountable lapses in style, but it also features some extraordinarily fine prose. Although its attempts at humor are frequently feeble and the portrayal of some characters unconvincing, *The World in the Evening* nevertheless maintains real interest throughout. In addition, it pioneers in a genuinely felt expression of homosexual militancy and in a famous articulation of a homosexual aesthetic, "High and Low Camp."[2]

If *The World in the Evening* is a relative failure, it is an honorable one, and the relativity of its failure must be measured in terms of the ambitiousness of

what it attempts. The book explores the subject that
John Donne announces in "The Progresse of the
Soule," the poem from which Isherwood's title is
taken:

> I sing the progresse of a deathlesse soule,
> Whom Fate, which God made, but doth not con-
>   troule,
> Plac'd in most shapes;
> . . . . .
> And the great world to his aged evening
> From infant morne, through noone I draw.[3]

The World in the Evening traces the journeys of its
worldly, self-absorbed protagonist from egoism to
spiritual awareness and from world-weariness to
commitment.

The novel opens in 1941 with a section entitled
"An End." Stephen Monk, a wealthy thirty-seven-
year-old Anglo-American, discovers the infidelity of
his second wife, Jane, at a Hollywood party. He im-
pulsively flees Los Angeles, "this antiseptic, heartless, hateful neon mirage of a city," and returns to
Dolgelly, Pennsylvania, to his family mansion, Tawelfan, a name that in Welsh means "The Quiet
Place." Once there he feels suffocated by the pro-
tective love of his Quaker courtesy relative and foster mother, Aunt Sarah, and he decides to flee
again; but as he attempts to leave, he is run down by
a truck that he probably could have avoided.

In the second section, "Life and Letters,"
Stephen recuperates from his accident and reviews
his past life, principally by rereading the letters of
his dead first wife, a well-known English novelist
named Elizabeth Rydal. He is nursed by Gerda
Mannheim, a German refugee who worries over the
fate of her anti-Nazi husband, now probably in a
concentration camp, and he is visited by his doctor,

Charles Kennedy, and his doctor's lover, a lapsed Quaker artist, Bob Wood.

In flashbacks initiated by Elizabeth's letters and by his own trancelike meditations, Stephen recounts the circumstances of his marriage at the age of twenty-two to a woman twelve years his senior. In the course of the marriage, they travel around the world. Elizabeth suffers a miscarriage and failing health. The couple becomes involved with a young homosexual, Michael Drummond, who falls in love with Stephen only to be betrayed by him. After Elizabeth's death, Stephen marries Jane Armstrong, an American with whom he had had an affair during Elizabeth's last illness.

In "A Beginning," the novel's final section, set in January 1942, Stephen returns to Tawelfan after a three-month stay in New York. He learns that Gerda's husband, Peter, has escaped from a concentration camp to the safety of Switzerland. He spends an evening with Charles Kennedy and Bob Wood, who has enlisted in the navy, and comes to a new understanding of Elizabeth's limitations as a novelist. Sarah surprises him with the revelation of her unrequited love for his long-dead father. In the final scene, he and Jane meet for the first time since their divorce and promise to remain friends. Both at peace with himself and committed to the world, Stephen has joined a civilian ambulance unit and is scheduled for duty as a driver in North Africa.

Stephen Monk is among Isherwood's most fascinating characters. Guilty of numerous acts of betrayal and motivated by selfishness and weakness, he nevertheless evokes sympathy rather than scorn. This reaction occurs at least in part because his failures are narrated retrospectively and because he acknowledges his guilt. More fundamentally, however, Stephen arouses sympathy as a result of the complex attractiveness that is central to his character.

After one shocking exhibition of Stephen's unkindness, Elizabeth warns him, "you have the power to hurt," alluding to Shakespeare's Sonnet 94. This sonnet, like many others addressed to the cruel but beautiful young man of the Shakespearean sequence, is simultaneously a bitter indictment and a compliment. Its final lines, "For sweetest things turn sourest by their deeds;/Lilies that fester smell far worse than weeds,"[4] perfectly captures the complex ambiguity of feeling that Stephen himself evokes. His essential attractiveness functions both to mitigate his unattractive traits and to underline them.

As with the young man in Shakespeare's sonnet, Stephen's sins are as much sins of omission as of commission. He uses his passivity to effect changes without having to accept responsibility for them. For instance, he selfishly manipulates Elizabeth into giving up her London literary friends by contriving to make it appear that she has been selfish in wanting them in the first place. He encourages Michael to fall in love with him and then relies on Elizabeth to break off the affair. He burdens her with his dependency, even as she struggles with her own fears of death.

Stephen's manipulation of Jane is equally ugly. When he feels "miserable and trapped and resentful" at the prospect of a child, he maneuvers her into obtaining an abortion and then declares, "I swear I never imagined . . . ." Although he has also been unfaithful in the course of their marriage, he allows Jane to accept responsibility for its dissolution. When he discovers her with Roy Griffin, he feels "a great, almost agonizing upsurge of glee, of gleeful relief." He even finds himself sexually excited, "thinking of them together; two mating giants filling the dwarf world of the doll's house, and nearly bursting it apart with their heavings and writhings."

Stephen's excitement at the memory of Jane and Roy in the doll's house is an indication of the infantilism of his sexual imagination. Like so many of Isherwood's Truly Weak Men, he suffers from an immaturity rooted in a mother fixation. Gerda tells him, "People will always be kind to you, Stephen. You can make them feel sorry for you, with your look like a little boy." When he asks Jane to marry him, she pointedly observes, "What you need, Stephen, is a mother or a nurse."

Stephen's mother fixation is strikingly emphasized in the scene in which he and Elizabeth agree to marry. Fearful of rejection, he forces her to declare her love first; he buries his face in a pillow and starts "to cry like a baby," while Elizabeth bends over him, maternally stroking his hair. Stephen's sexual immaturity is also suggested by his description of the infantile sensations he feels when he goes to bed with Michael for the first time: "In the darkness I remembered the adolescent, half-angry pleasure of wrestling with boys at school. And then, later, there was a going even further back, into the nursery sleep of childhood with its teddy bear, or of puppies or kittens in a basket, wanting only the warmness of anybody."

Stephen's egotism and dependency, as well as his immaturity, are fully illustrated in his relationship with Michael. A handsome, lonely, hero-worshipping ex-public-school boy, Michael functions for Stephen as "a looking glass of the most flattering kind." Stephen exploits Michael's affection and then cruelly repulses it by pretending that "it simply isn't important." When Stephen initiates their second sexual bout, he rationalizes his "shameless physical itch, transforming it into a big noble generous gesture, a gift of princely charity from myself, who had everything, to Michael, who had nothing." Unfortunately, Michael interprets Stephen's selfishly motivated and condescending gesture as a commitment of love.

Michael bravely confronts Elizabeth with the news of his affair with Stephen, telling her that he and Stephen are going away together. Elizabeth, who understands her young husband very well and knows his dependency on her, is unperturbed: "The reasons why Stephen wouldn't leave me for you—or anybody else—certainly aren't ones that I can be proud of. They're actually quite humiliating—or would be, if I hadn't lived with them for so long." When Stephen refuses to confirm his commitment, Michael leaves, crushed and embittered. He tells Elizabeth, "I'm not sure I'll ever be able to believe in anyone again."

Significantly, however, Michael does recover his faith. When Stephen and he meet again in 1937, shortly after Elizabeth's death, he is a mature and committed individual. In contrast, Stephen is rootlessly drifting through a purposeless existence on the Riviera. Now a member of the International Brigade who has been slightly wounded in the Spanish Civil War, Michael is no longer infatuated with Stephen. His new confidence and self-possessed maturity make Stephen "more than usually ashamed of the life I was living." Although grieving at the death of his lover in the war, Michael is yet able to view Stephen's "miserable mess" with compassion. "I can see you aren't happy," he tells Stephen, "I wish there was something I could do about it. But there isn't. I've found that out. You

have to work your way out of these things by yourself."

Stephen's eventual ability to work his way out
of his unhappiness is motivated by his awareness of
the pain of hunger beneath everything and his consequent need to discover the "deathlesse soule"
within him. Even in "The End," when he is most
fully oppressed by a sense of despair, he discovers
that the "absolute otherness" of the desert landscape—"the sort of super-spectacle which makes
some people think of God or Michaelangelo, and
which others find merely disgusting and dull because it seems to exclude their egos so completely"—makes him "almost happy."

In *The World in the Evening*, Isherwood casts
Stephen's spiritual journey in the familiar language
of Western religion and psychology, wisely avoiding the esoterica of Vedantic terminology; but the
novel illustrates the Vedantist belief that the secret
of happiness lies in escape from the ego and in discovery of the *Atman*, the God in man, the universal
consciousness. The specific choice of a Quaker
background for Stephen, Sarah, and Bob Wood may
have been motivated by Isherwood's observation
that "the Society of Friends is, as far as I am aware,
the Christian sect which comes closest to agreement with the teachings of Vedanta."[5]

Stephen's meditative trances lead to his fullest
early awareness of the *Atman* within him. Through
meditation he momentarily escapes the bondage of
the ego. As he lies in his convalescent bed, all the
circumstantial facts of his life "seemed to be scat-
tered around me, like the furniture of the room, all
simultaneously present . . . . Everything particular
was on the outside; and what was aware of this was
a simple consciousness that had no name, no face,

no identity of any kind." With genuine remorse, he acknowledges his past failures. But his consciousness refuses to wallow in the neurotic guilt of the ego: "It knew no feelings, except the feeling of being itself; and that was the deepest, quietest, most mysterious kind of happiness."

By the end of the novel, this happiness is integrated into the entire fabric of Stephen's life. The "black stinking bog" of his hatred is drained. Even while "lying in this sweaty bed and smelling like a garbage dump inside this cast," he feels free. He knows "that everything's going to be all right. And I'm not miserable and dreary and scared, any more." He describes his transformation as "a sort of miracle." Crucial to the miracle is the guidance Stephen receives from others, particularly from Elizabeth and Sarah.

In the book's final section, Sarah tells Stephen, "Whatever you do, you'll be guided." She also recalls some lines from William Penn: "They that love beyond the world cannot be separated by it. Death cannot kill what never dies . . . . If absence be not death, neither is theirs. Death is but crossing the world, as friends do the seas; they live in one another still." The relationship these lines describe perfectly fits Elizabeth's function in the book. As one who loves beyond the world, she transcends death to become a guiding force in the spiritual growth of her husband.

From the novel's very beginning, Stephen turns to the dead Elizabeth as a source of counsel. As he travels in the night sky across the desert on his flight to Tawelfan, he tells her, "Now I'm going to need you more than ever. I hope you know how much I need you and love you. Without you, I'm lost." He even attributes to her ghostly influence the accident that could have been avoided and that immobilizes him for ten weeks of introspective soul-searching: "Now I knew exactly what the accident was all about . . . . Very well, I told her. You finally succeeded. You stopped me from running any further."

Modeled on Katherine Mansfield and perhaps the most completely successful characterization in the novel, Elizabeth is subtly drawn. In her letters and in the flashbacks they occasion, she emerges as a fully human example of sensitivity and courage. Her courage is especially manifest as she approaches death, desperately striving to overcome her fear of dying alone. In a letter to a friend, she admits, "I had inside me a terrified animal, a creature absolutely blind and deaf and senseless with fear." Significantly, she overcomes this fear through religious faith.

Elizabeth's faith is not that of conventional Christianity, however. She rejects "church-religion," for religionists "have turned their God into such a very constitutional monarch. They've smothered Him in deference and bowed Him practically out of existence." Her version of God she prefers to call "It." "I, like everything else," she comes to realize, "am much more essentially in It than in I." Her confidence that "there's a source of life within me—and that It can't be destroyed" sustains her as she faces death: "I shall not live on, but It will." She finds solace by escaping the terrified ego and embracing the impersonal God within her.

Elizabeth's examples of independence and faith are supplemented by those of Sarah. A far less successful characterization than Elizabeth, Sarah is too much a stock figure of selfless goodness to be completely convincing. Nevertheless, her restless involvement in good deeds and her unshakable faith help speed Stephen on his journeys toward spiritual enlightenment and social commitment. Her example of spiritual insight is experienced by Stephen both directly and indirectly.

Sarah's impact on Gerda teaches Stephen indirectly. Like Stephen, Gerda rejects Sarah's Quakerism, but the refugee nevertheless declares that "what Sarah believes, I believe . . . . Because it is *she* who believes, and not another." Gerda movingly recounts a moment of revelation when Sarah wordlessly comforted her: "The room gets very still. I cannot describe—but it is like when you are in a place with deep snow all around—so still. You feel only the stillness. And it was then that I knew . . . . It is all right—even if Peter is *not* safe—even if the worst happens, to him and to me. Suddenly, I knew that. Sarah made me know it." Similarly, when Sarah later tells Stephen of the power of love, even from beyond the grave, he too has a revelation: "I had an uncanny feeling—it was very close to fear—that I was somehow 'in the presence'—but of what? The whatever-it-was behind Sarah's eyes looked out at me through them, as if through the eye-holes in a mask. And its look meant: Yes, I am always here."

Stephen's discovery of the *Atman* leads to worldly commitment and to self-acceptance. When Elizabeth recognizes the God within her, she tells Stephen, "We only get afraid because we cling to things in the past or the future. If you stay in the present moment, you're never afraid, and you're safe—because that's always." By embracing the present, Stephen becomes a participant in life in a way he has never been before. At the beginning of the novel, for instance, the war exists for Stephen "merely as a loud, ugly appropriate background music for my expensive private hell." At the end, the war is a hell whose suffering he is committed to help alleviate as an ambulance driver.

All the subsidiary characters in the novel offer Stephen significant examples of commitment and of courage. Elizabeth's devotion to her art is finally recognized as having been important for its own sake, even if her novels no longer seem first-rate, for she pursued her writing in a spirit of nonattachment. Sarah's involvement in helping others rebukes Stephen's selfish egocentricity in his past life, as do Gerda's political commitment and suffering. Less obviously, Charles Kennedy and especially Bob Wood, who are often thought to be peripheral characters, also contribute to Stephen's journey toward active participation in life.

Their importance resides in Bob's militancy, his understanding of the political dimensions of being homosexual in a world that systematically falsifies the gay experience. The angriest of Isherwood's gay characters, Bob quickly reveals his homosexuality to Stephen, describing himself as "a professional criminal." When Stephen mouths a liberally tolerant caution—suggesting that the young man should not be "so aggressive. That's what puts people against you"—Bob bitterly attacks the heterosexual majority for its failure to accept the gay minority: "Maybe we ought to put people against us. Maybe we're just too damned tactful. People just ignore us, most of the time, and we let them. We encourage them to. So the whole business never gets discussed, and the laws never get changed."

This passionate outburst reveals the extent of Bob's alienation. He has rejected his Quaker heritage because the Friends refuse to confront the issue of gay oppression, and he has been criminalized by the larger society. Like Michael Drummond, his chief characteristic is a "quality of loneliness." He would like to "march down the street with a banner, singing 'We're queer because we're queer because we're queer because we're queer.' " But this protest, wildly unlikely in 1941, is impossible: his lover Charles, a Jew who has changed his name, "is sick of belonging to these whining militant minorities."

Like many of Isherwood's characters, Bob is torn between apparently incompatible needs. On the one hand, casually accepting his homosexuality as part of the wholeness of personality, he feels a need to assert his individuality. On the other hand, he has a deeply felt need to find acceptance. Charles's prescription for Bob's dilemma is the improbable creation of "Quaker Camp." But, tellingly, the solution Bob finds for himself is political at base.

At the end of the novel, Bob joins the navy, declining noncombatant status as a conscientious objector because "if they declared war on the queers—I'd fight." His motives are not conventionally patriotic: "Compared with this business of being queer, and the laws against us, and the way we're pushed around even in peacetime—this war hardly seems to concern me at all." But he refuses to accept exemption from military service on the basis of his homosexuality, "because what they're claiming is that us queers are unfit for their beautiful pure Army and Navy—when they ought to be glad to have us."

The plight of Bob and Charles affords Stephen an opportunity to escape his own self-absorption and to respond empathetically to others. Perhaps motivated at least in part by a desire to atone for his mistreatment of Michael, Stephen counsels Bob and Charles on their relationship; he agrees to act as "umpire" in the pair's disagreements by declaring, "For you, I'd break one of my necks any time." He promises Bob that if war were declared on homosexuals he would be "one of your spies." And he encourages Sarah to act on her need to tell Charles "not to mind too much if we haven't understood him as we should have. . . . I fear that Charles feels cut off from us now and bitterly lonely; and we refuse him any word of comfort. We refuse to recognize what it was that he and Bob shared together."

The World in the Evening is a *Bildungsroman,* a novel of education. It records Stephen Monk's development from an egocentric, perpetual adolescent into a responsible adult. Significantly, it posits a connection between spiritual illumination and worldly action. In escaping the constricting bonds of the ego, Stephen not only discovers an impersonal God within him but he also learns concern for others and commitment to life. As a consequence, he grows beyond egotistical guilt-mongering and affirms himself. "Do you know something, Jane," he asks in the book's final line, "I really do forgive myself, from the bottom of my heart?"

The novel is also a love story large enough to include varieties of love as diverse as its characters: the love of Elizabeth and Stephen, of Sarah and Stephen's father, of Michael and his soldier friend, of Charles and Bob, of Gerda and Peter. The value of love permeates the entire book. When Sarah explains to Stephen her relationship with his father, she remarks, "When one really loves, these situations have a way of solving themselves, I think." For all the couples in the book, love is a saving grace; and "they that love beyond the world" are redeemed. They gain an immortality that concretely impinges on the eternal present.

The World in the Evening is a seriously flawed

novel. Quite apart from its occasional lapses of style
and the wooden characterization of several minor
figures, it suffers from overschematization. The
spiritual affirmation seems to be imposed on the
characters rather than to develop naturally from
their predicaments. Moreover, the happy endings
for nearly all the characters smack of sentimentality.
Thus the bleak hopelessness of *The Memorial* is finally more convincing than the happy solutions of
The World in the Evening.

Still, despite its disappointments, the later
novel remains fascinating. The opening section is
superbly written, and the whole is of absorbing interest. In the haunting portraits of Elizabeth Rydal
and Stephen Monk, the book sketches the landscape of the soul, movingly affirming the power of
those who "love beyond the world." In addition, the
novel suggests a nexus between the soul and society. An ambitious exploration of the spiritual quest,
The World in the Evening unobtrusively translates
Vedantic wisdom into a familiar Western idiom.

6

∿∿∿∿∿∿∿∿∿∿∿∿∿∿∿∿∿∿∿∿∿∿∿∿∿∿∿∿∿∿∿∿∿∿∿∿

A Continuity
of Consciousness:
Down There on a Visit

If *The World in the Evening* is Isherwood's most problematic novel, *Down There on a Visit* may be his most complex. Published in 1962, the book suffers from few of the stylistic lapses that mar its predecessor. Returning to the namesake narrator of the Berlin stories and of *Prater Violet* and employing the loosely connected structural organization of *Goodbye to Berlin, Down There on a Visit* constitutes a radical reinterpretation of its author's past. The material that the book treats is familiar, and its concerns are consistent with those of the earlier novels, yet it is finally an unsparing assessment of the human condition. Preoccupied with the failure of commitment, it is the most deeply disturbing of Isherwood's works.

The use of the namesake narrator in *Down There on a Visit* is far more complex than it is in the earlier novels. Divided into four distinct episodes covering the time span from 1928 through 1953, the book achieves unity primarily through the continuing and developing presence of the narrator. Early in the novel, Isherwood as author intrudes into the narrative to draw a crucial distinction between himself and his namesake: "We still share the same skeleton, but its outer covering has altered so much that I doubt if he would recognize me on the street.

We have in common the label of our name, and a
continuity of consciousness; there has been no
break in the sequence of daily statements that I am
I. But *what* I am has refashioned itself throughout
the days and years, until now almost all that remains
constant is the mere awareness of being conscious."

This distinction helps to define the novel as an
inquiry into the protean self, and it establishes the
relativity of the self as a dominant motif. It places
the author in the present of 1962, looking back on
earlier versions of himself, each later version pre-
sumably more nearly identical to the author as he is
in 1962.

As an examination of the author's past from the
perspective of the present, *Down There on a Visit* is
the most insistently autobiographical of Isherwood's novels, each of which is firmly rooted in
his own experience. But as autobiography, *Down
There on a Visit* is adversely selective, and the developing portrait of the narrator comes to seem like
self-laceration, creating a troubling barrier between
the reader and the narrator. Paradoxically, the barrier functions as one source of the book's extraordinary power.

The novel's first section is entitled "Mr. Lancaster." Set in 1928, immediately following the
publication of *All the Conspirators*, the episode recounts Christopher's visit to a North German city at
the invitation of a distant family relation. A pom-
pous businessman, Mr. Lancaster alternates between ignoring the young Christopher and assum-
ing an unearned avuncular pose. Alexander
Lancaster is a lonely and disappointed man who has
lived "too long inside his sounding-box, listening to
his own reverberations, his epic song of himself."
His invitation to Christopher may represent an attempt to arouse the young man's curiosity and to

establish desperately needed human contact. But with the arrogance of youth, Christopher believes that "everyone over forty belonged . . . to an alien tribe, hostile by definition but in practice ridiculous rather than formidable." He fails to recognize Mr. Lancaster as anything but absurd. He later learns of the older man's suicide.

The second episode, "Ambrose," is set in 1933. Accompanied by Waldemar, a carefree youth who in the "Mr. Lancaster" section had introduced him to German sexual freedom, Christopher leaves Berlin for the Greek island of St. Gregory, where Ambrose, an expatriate Englishman, is building a house. Described in terms suggesting saintliness and otherworldly absorption, Ambrose greets Christopher by announcing that he, the host, is dead, at least as far as England is concerned. At present, he presides over a disorderly ménage that includes a German bodyguard, Hans Schmidt; a dissipated English remittance man named Geoffrey; and several Greek boys, most notable among them the violent Aleko, who taunts Hans.

On the island, at least partly to tease the heterosexual chauvinist Geoffrey, Ambrose fantasizes about an imaginary homosexual kingdom. The homosexual idyll that Ambrose has created is soon disrupted by the unexpected arrival of Maria Constantinescu, a sexual adventuress who recognizes Christopher as a fellow "monster." After seducing Waldemar, she leaves the island with Geoffrey. Following a violent confrontation with Aleko, Hans also leaves, taking Waldemar with him. Eventually Christopher and Ambrose are left alone on the island, apart from an ever changing cast of Greek boys. They lead a life of indolence and disorientation. When Christopher decides to leave, he realizes that he belongs nowhere.

"Waldemar," the third section, is set in 1938 at the height of the Sudetenland crisis. En route to England from France, Christopher meets a Communist friend, Dorothy, and discovers that she has fallen in love with Waldemar, whom she romanticizes as a worker and for whom she feels an intense sexual attraction. After an embarrassing confrontation with suspicious immigration officials, Waldemar is able to obtain only a limited visa. In England, Dorothy's disapproving upper-middle-class family treats him like a servant, and eventually the couple's relationship disintegrates.

Meanwhile Christopher is paralyzed by the political crisis and by his dread of war. He reexamines his political commitments and discovers that they are meaningless. After the Munich agreement lessens the immediate threat of war, Christopher resolves that he will leave England for America and that "as far as I am concerned, nothing, nothing, nothing is worth a war." Waldemar unsuccessfully pleads with Christopher to take him to America and then departs for Germany.

The final episode, "Paul," is set mainly in Hollywood during the war. Now a disciple of the guru Augustus Parr, Christopher is a successful screen writer. He becomes involved with a male prostitute, Paul, who confesses his spiritual despair and suicidal impulses. With the guidance of Augustus, Christopher and Paul embark on a regimen of spiritual and physical discipline. Possessing an enormous natural capacity for spiritual involvement, Paul devotes himself to asceticism, a devotion that is interrupted by a young girl's false accusation of sexual advances and by enforced service in a forestry camp for conscientious objectors.

After the war, Christopher travels to Europe, where he is reunited with Waldemar, now married and living with his wife and son in the Russian zone of occupied Berlin. Christopher ignores Waldemar's hint that he sponsor the family's emigration to the United States. Leaving Berlin, he visits Paul in Paris, where the former prostitute is now an opium addict. When Christopher timidly offers to smoke one pipe of opium with his friend, Paul scorns him as a "tourist": "You know, you really *are* a tourist, to your bones. I bet you're always sending postcards with 'Down here on a visit' on them." Later, Christopher learns that Paul, after having cured himself of his drug addiction, has died from a heart attack.

The four episodes of *Down There on a Visit* chronicle Christopher's search for meaning in life as well as his repeated failures of commitment. In broad outline, the novel charts his growth toward maturity, his escape from self-defeating egoism. But perhaps as an overreaction against the sentimental journey of Stephen Monk in *The World in the Evening*, Isherwood refuses to dramatize the narrator's actual arrival into maturity. Indeed, he focuses the novel's irony most devastatingly against Christopher, the character who is treated least empathetically.

In contrast to the unsparing exposure of Christopher's heartlessness is the compassion with which all the other major characters are treated. As well as being presented with insight and understanding, however, each of these characters in turn is revealed as a mirror of Christopher's potentiality.

Although Christopher is in many ways a polar opposite to the puritanical Alexander Lancaster, whose favorite poet is William Watson—a minor Victorian who attempted to purge British art of homosexual influence after the Oscar Wilde scandal of 1895—they share a basic indifference to others.

Both men are preoccupied with creating epic songs of themselves, and the callow Christopher's self-absorption deafens him to the older man's pleas for help. Mr. Lancaster's suicide represents an option that Christopher himself might choose if he remains ego-bound.

Ambrose's extreme alienation also mirrors Christopher's inability to find a place where he belongs. Ambrose's retreat from the larger world into a Mortmere-like universe of his own creation—into a self-imposed death—offers another possibility for Christopher, but one that he is too weak to accept. Significantly, Ambrose's retreat is not wholly voluntary. Permanently scarred by the trashing of his rooms at Cambridge by a group of undergraduate hearties, he has been evicted from a series of lodgings. "I never want to move," he explains. "But they won't let me stay—*anywhere....* That's what makes most places utterly impossible—the people. They're so completely hateful. They want everybody to conform to their beastly narrow little way of looking at things. And if one happens not to, one's treated as something unspeakable."

Compared to "one of Shakespeare's exiled kings," Ambrose resembles Prospero in *The Tempest,* especially in his desire to create a brave new world of his own imagining. Ambrose's fantasy of a self-created homosexual kingdom is especially revealing as a parody of the unjust reality that provokes his alienation:

Of course, when we do get into power, we shall have to begin by reassuring everybody. We must make it clear that there'll be absolutely no reprisals. Actually, they'll be amazed to find how tolerant we are.... I'm afraid we shan't be able to make heterosexuality actually legal, at first—there'd be too much of an outcry.... But meanwhile it'll be winked at, of course, as long as it's practiced

in decent privacy. I think we shall even allow a few bars
to be opened for people with those unfortunate tenden-
cies, in certain quarters of the larger cities.

This comic fantasy cannot be taken wholly seriously, yet it is of great importance, embodying as it
does the homosexual's bitterness at being excluded
from the larger society. Moreover, the fantasy also
betrays Ambrose's hidden desire for involvement in
the world, albeit at a level beyond the reality that he
finds unacceptable. Indeed, it is Ambrose's awareness of the injustice and cruelty of the existing majority culture that both fuels his parody and accounts for his attempt to create an alternate world.

At the end of the section, when the island community has been mostly abandoned, Christopher
asks Ambrose, "Don't you mind being alone here—
with nobody but the boys?" The haunting reply—
"But one's always alone, ducky. Surely you know
that"—indicates Ambrose's existential isolation, indicts the dominant culture for its failure to extend a
sense of community beyond its "beastly narrow little way of looking at things," and perhaps even
questions the possibility of meaningful community.
But whereas Ambrose has the strength of character
to transform his isolation into anarchic self-suffi-
ciency, Christopher does not. Under the fierce discipline of Ambrose's commitment to a vision of living death, Christopher's ego disintegrates into the
chaos of disorientation. Christopher finally decides
against the renunciation of life; he discovers in his
shaving mirror "a look in my eyes which hadn't
been there before": a glimpse of the inner need that
propels him toward the spiritual involvement of the
final section.

While the "Ambrose" episode provides Christopher the opportunity of withdrawal from the

world into a disorienting timeless fantasy, the "Waldemar" section depicts him sickeningly mired in the immediate present of political crisis. By now a successful writer whose work is "chic, not vulgarly famous," Christopher describes himself as possessing "the arrogance of Lawrence of Arabia and the subtlety of Talleyrand." He has proved himself by successfully playing the game of "The Others": "all the headmasters of the schools I went to, all the clergymen I have ever known, all reactionary politicians, newspaper editors, journalists, and most women over forty. Ever since I've been able to talk and read they have been telling me the rules of their game. And they've been insinuating, until lately, with sneering smiles, 'But, of course, *you* could never play it.'"

Despite his success, however, Christopher is desperately unhappy. His inner emptiness is often expressed in bitter denunciations of religion and in dogmatic assertions that he has no soul. One such outburst prompts his friend Hugh Weston to warn, "Careful! Careful! If you keep going on like that, my dear, you'll have *such* a conversion, one of these days!"

This third section intertwines Christopher's personal despair with the political crisis of the moment and with the dissolving relationship of Dorothy and Waldemar. Dorothy clings tenaciously to communism as a source of meaning for her life, but Christopher finds all his political commitments hollow. Waldemar's deterioration is especially frightening, for he too is a mirror in which Christopher recognizes himself. The only character besides Christopher who appears in all four sections, Waldemar is initially described as "quite beautiful, in a high-cheekboned, Gothic style. He looked like one of the carved stone angels in the cathedral." But his angelic beauty fades quickly, and in the section bearing his name he is a cruel opportunist, "for the first time in his life, capable of hurting others."

As a victim of English snobbery and of the chaotic European political climate, Waldemar also mirrors Christopher's reaction to England and to public life. Despising England as the bastion of The Others, Christopher embraces the humane individualism of E. M. (Forster), "the antiheroic hero, with his straggly straw mustache, his light, gay blue baby eyes and his elderly stoop. . . . He and his books and what they stand for are all that is truly worth saving. . . ." Ironically, however, E. M. "advises us to live as if we were immortal," yet Christopher can cope with the political crisis only by grasping at a phrase from Balzac: *"un jour sans lendemain,* a day without a morrow." Trapped in the transient present, he fills his life with tomorrowless sex and tomorrowless promises.

As a result of his obsession with the political uncertainty of 1938, Christopher discovers his fear of war. He decides to abandon England altogether and embrace the private life in America, where he will "try to unlearn my madness and forget my ancestors and become sane again." This decision, born of despair but nursed by hope, marks a crucial stage in Christopher's developing maturity, for it signals a commitment to the future and to a new beginning. Significantly, however, it is accompanied by personal betrayal, as Christopher refuses to aid Waldemar. The latter's accusation—"You're like the others. You tell me not to go back to Germany. But you won't help"—reverberates with irony. For all Christopher's denunciations of The Others, he is actually just like them. He abandons the despairing present for a hopeful future, but in doing so he betrays the private life he embraces.

As the final section opens, Christopher has escaped from the despair of "Waldemar." As he admits, he is still not happy. But his life has acquired new purpose through a fragile religious commitment nurtured by the guru Augustus Parr. Christopher's belief in the *Atman,* "this thing that's inside us and yet isn't us," is primarily the result of his personal response to Parr, a response similar to Gerda's reaction to Sarah in *The World in the Evening.* "I believe in Parr's belief," he reveals. The basis of his pacifist stance is also largely personal: Waldemar might be an enemy soldier. Tellingly, Christopher's new religious orientation is itself a reflection of his ego. "Now at last," he comments, "I'm playing *my* game, not the game of The Others."

The incompleteness of Christopher's commitment to the new "game" is exposed by the legendary Paul, "the most expensive male prostitute in the world." The relationship of Paul and Christopher is the most complex in the novel. Christopher responds to Paul with a convincingly human mixture of love, concern, petulance, and especially jealousy. His jealousy results largely from his recognition that the very excessiveness of Paul's character mocks his own timidity and pretentiousness. When Paul shows up at his apartment in dire spiritual need, Christopher arranges a meeting with Augustus. The guru perceives in Paul what he defines as "dynamic despair. The kind that makes dangerous criminals, and very occasionally, saints."

Augustus describes Paul's response to meditation in terms that underline the limitations of Christopher's religious experience: "What was so enormously impressive was the completeness with which [Paul] gave himself to the experience. Self-knowledge is impossible for most of us because we can't push aside this thing that stands in the way of it; but here one felt that the entire ego-sheath had been sloughed off. Do you know, Christopher, his face—it was suddenly the face of a pre-adolescent boy? One was in the presence of true innocence."

Hearing of Paul's spiritual potentiality, Christopher feels "meanly jealous" of his "spiritual superior." He is able to repress his envy only by reflecting that "at the end, Augustus had made everything all right again by appointing me Paul's savior, which left me feeling wonderfully benevolent toward Paul and quite a bit of a saint myself."

Paul moves into Christopher's apartment and the two of them lead a monastic life, helping each other practice almost total abstinence. Here again the fullness of Paul's commitment contrasts with the incompleteness of Christopher's. Christopher describes this period as "one of the happiest" of his life, yet there is a destructiveness in his character that wills his and Paul's failure. Christopher later admits at least partial responsibility for the events at the retreat that culminate in a preadolescent girl's false accusation against Paul: "Part of me—the minority, certainly, but desperate and quite ruthless— wanted to precipitate a scandal in which every- thing—the entire life I had been leading—would come to an end. The minority neither knew nor cared exactly what the long-term results of its coun- terrevolution would be. It simply hoped to find some advantage and opportunity for itself among the ruins."

As the novel concludes, both Christopher and Paul retreat from their devotion to Vedantism. When the two meet after Paul's medical discharge from the forestry service, Christopher explains, "I still believe what I used to. Only now I don't feel I have to be so puritanical about it. It doesn't seem to me to be so much a matter of keeping rules any more. Of course, I admit there have to be *some* rules. But the rules aren't what's really important. What's really important is ... 'love.'" Paul's response punctures Christopher's posturing: "'*Really*, honey!' he interrupted. 'Spare me these rationalizations, *please*! All I can say is, you'd better start making up your mind before it's too late. Either be a proper monk, or a dirty old man.' " As always, Paul is uncompromising.

Paul's rejection of Vedantism is a rejection of "autohypnotism and professional goodness." "I'm sick of trying to imagine I feel things," he declares. "I just want to *know*." He does not doubt the genuineness of Augustus's belief—with affectionate campiness, he remarks, "Miss Parr is still the biggest saint in show business"—but he seeks direct spiritual knowledge rather than feeling. This quest leads him first to the rational knowledge of psychoanalysis and finally to the intuitive knowledge of the drug experience. That Paul seeks intuitive knowledge is an important clue to his spiritual seriousness, for as Aldous Huxley writes in his introduction to the Prabhavananda-Isherwood translation of the Bhagavad Gita, "human beings are capable not merely of knowing *about* the Divine Ground by inference; they can also realize its existence by a direct intuition, superior to discursive reasoning. This immediate knowledge unites the knower with that which is known."[1]

The significance of Paul's drug addiction is somewhat obscured as a result of Isherwood's last-minute decision to excise an important scene at the very end of the novel. This scene, which Isherwood deleted after the book was in galley proofs and which he later published in *Exhumations* as "A Visit to Anselm Oakes," links Paul to a literary tradition of sinner-saints who consciously immerse themselves in evil in order to discover good.[2] In "A Visit to Anselm Oakes," Paul initiates Christopher into a drug-induced state of timelessness that terrifies him. Paul remarks, "Augustus knows the score all right . . . . The only mistake he makes is trying to tell other people. You can't. Everyone has to find out for himself. If you talk about it, it's nothing at all—just another lousy word . . . . Eternity."[3]

Even without the excised scene, however, Paul's drug addiction at the end of *Down There on a Visit* functions to emphasize the totality of his commitment to the spiritual quest. When Christopher visits him in Paris, he describes Paul as "Dorian Gray arisen from the tomb." "There was an air about him of being somehow preserved and, at the same time, purified," Christopher remarks. "Indeed, he was marvelously, uncannily beautiful." Paul tells Christopher that he plans to cure his drug addiction "when I've found out all I want to know." That Paul does succeed in curing himself may be testimony that he does learn all he wants to know, and his death may rightly be regarded as the apotheosis of a sinner-saint.[4]

In contrast to Paul, Christopher remains a tourist, "Down here on a visit," never sharing the private hells of others, always shirking full involvement. Appropriately, the novel ends with Christopher preoccupied with guilt at refusing to sponsor the escape of Waldemar and his family from East Berlin. But notwithstanding his failure to achieve maturity, Christopher has grown in the novel. His journey from youthful callousness through monstrous curiosity and neurotic worldliness culminates in his arrival as a self-aware, partially committed individual with the potential for further growth.

Although it is Isherwood's most disturbing novel, *Down There on a Visit* is informed by an optimistic vision. Its optimism resides in the continuity of consciousness that links the unsparing author and his still-developing narrator. If at the end of the book Christopher is still a tourist, his future self, the author, is not. Like *The World in the Evening*, *Down There on a Visit* is a *Bildungsroman*. The difference is that the latter novel avoids the sentimentality of the former by refusing to depict the narrator's emergence into full maturity.

Down There on a Visit is among Isherwood's major achievements. The "Ambrose" and "Waldemar" sections are flawlessly constructed and the "Paul" episode only slightly less impressive. Written with restraint and concision and with full mastery of characterization, the novel as a whole is a remarkable study of the protean self. The autobiographical elements foster a deeply disturbing reaction to the book as an unappetizing exercise in self-laceration, but the continuity of consciousness between narrator and author also contributes to the novel's enormous power as an unsentimental dissection of the past. Although it suffers from the Saint Augustine syndrome of magnifying prior sins in order to stress the changes wrought by religious conversion, *Down There on a Visit* is nevertheless lightened by humor and informed by optimism. As Brian Finney notes, it constitutes "an extraordinary return to Isherwood's powers of the late thirties."[5] Moreover, in its concern with the problem of commitment, *Down There on a Visit* anticipates its even greater successor, *A Single Man*.

〇〇

The Waters of the Pool:
A Single Man

A Single Man is the masterpiece of Isherwood's maturity. The novel combines technical perfection and
broad vision, humanistic understanding and spiritual perspective. It is concerned with death and decay and with the disparity between the body and
the spirit. Yet it is frequently humorous and never
sentimental or depressing. Dealing with universal
themes of commitment and grief, alienation and isolation, the book concretely explores the minority
sensibility, presenting the homosexual predicament
as a faithful mirror of the human condition. Masterfully balancing worldly and religious points of
view, *A Single Man* is among the most undervalued
novels of our time.

Published in 1964, *A Single Man* is the most
concentrated and narrowly circumscribed of
Isherwood's books, limited as it is to one day in the
life of a single character in a single city. The day
begins with the protagonist's awakening in his bed,
and it ends with his falling asleep in the same bed.
Although the outward events that the novel records
are unremarkable, the day turns out to be significant. And in tracing this one day in the life of an
unlikely hero, Isherwood, with characteristically
deceptive ease, casually exposes the entire fabric of
a single man's existence and the full texture of life

in twentieth-century America. His portrait of Los
Angeles in the early 1960s is comparable in irony
and insight to his portraits of Berlin in the early
1930s.

The novel follows a day in the life of George, a
middle-aged and lonely expatriate Briton who
teaches English at San Tomas State College in Los
Angeles. He is a homosexual who lives alone following the death of Jim, his lover of many years.
Wracked by grief and tormented by the children of
his philistine neighbors, he is near the end of his
endurance. In the course of the novel, George's
daily routine is assiduously catalogued, from his
first moments of consciousness through his last
waking thoughts.

After breakfast, he distractedly drives via freeway to the college, where he meets students,
teaches a class, and converses with colleagues.
When he leaves the campus, he stops at a hospital to
visit Doris, a friend who several years ago had se-
duced Jim and who is now dying of cancer. De-
pressed by the visit, he makes an unscheduled de-
tour to the gymnasium, where he works out more
vigorously than usual. Leaving the gym, he impul-
sively drives through the hills overlooking the city.
He stops the car "and looks out over Los Angeles
like a sad Jewish prophet of doom, as he takes a
leak." He drives on to a supermarket, where he is
overcome with despair and suddenly decides to accept a dinner invitation extended earlier by Charlotte, a fellow expatriate, "like him . . . a survivor."

After a sentimental and alcoholic evening with
Charlotte, whom he calls Charley, George decides
to walk down to the Starboard Side, a bar where he
and Jim met in 1946. At the bar, he is surprised to
find Kenny, a flirtatious student who dares George
to a swim in the ocean. During the "baptism of the

surf," George feels himself purified by the water. Cold and wet, George and Kenny walk to George's house where, after much conversation, George eventually passes out from an excess of alcohol. Kenny puts him to bed and then leaves. George awakens, masturbates, decides to fly to Mexico for Christmas, and then drifts off into a sleep that might also be his death.

The key to the novel's extraordinary power resides in its brilliant narrative technique. Narrated dispassionately in the third person, the novel presents George with what at first appears to be clinical detachment, as a kind of biological exhibit to be contemplated by narrator and reader alike. As the book proceeds, George develops from a depersonalized object—"Obediently, it washes, shaves, brushes its hair"—into a "three-quarters-human thing," and finally, into full humanity. Concurrently, the narrator becomes increasingly less clinical and detached, and the distance between him and George gradually narrows, until the reversion to medical terminology in the final scene.

This narrative technique functions complexly to accomplish a number of effects. First of all, the distance between narrator and protagonist helps establish the book's double vision, its simultaneous concern with the mundane and the transcendent. Examining George as a biological specimen, the narrator seems to speak with more than human authority. By observing George *sub specie aeternitatis*, he unobtrusively underlines the novel's body-spirit dichotomy. And because the narrator frequently addresses the reader directly, the book becomes—in Paul Piazza's explanation—"a symbolic dialogue between the author as guru and the reader as a disciple meditating on the ephemera of George's day."[1]

Interestingly, the dispassionate narration also fosters the reader's identification with the alienated, homosexual hero. The narrator's persistent and flagrant invasions of George's privacy, even following him into the bathroom and frequently reporting on his bodily functions, create an enforced intimacy between reader and protagonist. However different the circumstances of George and any particular reader, the reader is still, like George, a mortal animal whose body is destined eventually to become "cousin to the garbage in the container on the back porch. Both will have to be carted away and disposed of, before too long." This recognition of a common mortality helps bridge all the barriers that separate the reader and the minority-conscious hero. As Jonathan Raban asks, "Dare we judge that decaying biological thing when it is we ourselves who may be George?"[2]

In *A Single Man*—this "masterpiece of a comic novel"[3]—Isherwood humorously and movingly captures the essence of homosexual resentment against a liberal society that routinely denies the validity of gay love. George is the most fully human of all Isherwood's homosexual characters, and the relationship of George and Jim gradually emerges to become the most deeply felt love story in all of Isherwood's fiction. George shares the alienation and anger of characters like Michael Drummond and Bob Wood in *The World in the Evening* and Ambrose in *Down There on a Visit*. But *A Single Man* more fully develops the context of gay oppression, especially in its more subtle and insidious forms, and places it within a still larger context of spiritual transcendence; and George's alienation finally yields both to a renewed commitment to life and to a new spiritual awareness.

The singleness of George reflects his alienation

as a homosexual as well as the essential isolation of the human condition. More specifically, George is single as the result of the loss of Jim. Early in the novel, the narrator records the pain of grief with poignant intensity: "And it is here, nearly every morning, that George, having reached the bottom of the stairs, has this sensation of suddenly finding himself on an abrupt, brutally broken off, jagged edge—as though the track had disappeared down a landslide. It is here that he stops short and knows, with a sick newness almost as though it were for the first time: Jim is dead. Is dead."

The obsession with and constant rediscovery of his loss cripple George, who at the beginning of the book is a "live dying creature" who "will struggle on and on until it drops. Not because it is heroic. It can imagine no alternative." George's continuing love for Jim invests the novel with great tenderness, as when George imagines his dead lover "lying opposite him at the other end of the couch, also reading; the two of them absorbed in their books yet so completely aware of each other's presence." But George's grief serves to isolate him and to chain him in memories. By the end of the day, however, he accepts the fact that "Jim is in the past, now" and concludes, "It is Now that he must find another Jim. Now that he must love. Now that he must live."

George's homosexuality is not merely an incidental aspect of his personality, as it might be in a novel less aware of the homophobia that afflicts American society. Homosexuality is the characteristic that most pervasively defines George's life. Constantly aware of being gay in a straight world, he reveals his minority consciousness most explicitly when he focuses on the issue of persecution in a classroom discussion of Aldous Huxley's *After Many a Summer*. "A minority," George says, "is only thought of as a minority when it constitutes some kind of threat to the majority, real or imaginary. And no threat is ever *quite* imaginary." He goes on to observe that the inevitable result of persecution is hatred: "While you're being persecuted, you hate what's happening to you, you hate the people who are making it happen, you're in a world of hate."

These characteristics of persecution are mirrored in George's own experience, as they were in the lives of Bob Wood and Ambrose. George attributes his neighbors' unease in the "kingdom of the good life upon earth," as he refers to the middle-class utopia that is Southern California, to the fear of nonconformity: "Among many other kinds of monster, George says, they are afraid of little me."

Like Ambrose, he expresses his hatred in comic fantasies of vengeance. As he drives along the freeway, he plans to form "Uncle George's" terrorist organization and kidnap the newspaper editor who has launched a vicious campaign against sex deviates, his staff writers, the police chief, the head of the vice squad, and the ministers who encourage the campaign. But another response to the oppression that George feels is the flipness and gentle parody of gay humor, as when he complains, "Why can't these modern writers stick to the old simple themes—such as, for example, boys?"

Rather than being subject to overt persecution, George most commonly experiences attitudes of condescending tolerance or studied indifference to his sexuality. He decides that his students probably guess that he is homosexual, but that the fact does not interest them: "They don't want to know about my feelings or my glands or anything below my neck. I could just as well be a severed head carried into the classroom to lecture to them from a dish."

He contrasts the attitude of his neighbor Mr. Strunk—who would, he thinks, "nail him down with a word. *Queer*, he doubtless growls"—with that of Mrs. Strunk, who is "trained in the new tolerance, the technique of annihilation by blandness. Out comes her psychology book—bell and candle are no longer necessary." Mrs. Strunk's position illustrates well Dennis Altman's observation that "the difference between tolerance and acceptance is very considerable, for tolerance is a gift extended by the superior to the inferior."[4] George's reply to her in his imaginary dialogue firmly rejects both her condescension and her psychology: "But your book is wrong . . . when it tells you that Jim is the substitute I found for a real son, a real kid brother, a real husband, a real wife. Jim wasn't a substitute for anything. And there is no substitute for Jim, if you'll forgive my saying so, anywhere."

George's isolation is emphasized by his decision not to share the news of Jim's death. He first learns of the accident from Jim's uncle, who even admitted "George's right to a small honorary share in the sacred family grief." But George refuses to betray any emotion to the uncle and declines an invitation to the funeral. Although Mrs. Strunk "would enjoy being sad about Jim" (in her liberal tolerance, she believes that a homosexual relationship "can sometimes be almost beautiful—particularly if one of the parties is already dead, or better yet, both"), George tells her merely that Jim will be remaining in the East indefinitely. Only with Charley does he share his grief. But after sobbing in her arms and accepting her comfort, George has second thoughts. He fears that he has made Jim "into a sob story for a skirt." Only when he realizes that "you

can't betray . . . a Jim, or a life with a Jim, even if
you try to" does he allow Charley to participate
fully in the ritual of grief.

George's singleness is particularly underscored
by his alienation from a homosexual community. Indeed, the absence of a viable gay community in the
days before the Stonewall riots and the gay activist
movements, when the homosexual minority is "one
that isn't organized and doesn't have any commit-
tees to defend it," may be one of the most significant factors in Isherwood's use of homosexuality as
a metaphor for the alienation endemic to the general human condition. At any rate, in *A Single Man*
George encounters no fellow homosexuals with
whom he might share a common identity. Only in
his visits to two women who know of his relationship with Jim is George free to be open about his
sexual orientation. But these visits, each in a different way, serve to shrink rather than to expand
George's sense of community.

His first visit is to Doris, who had once attempted to lure Jim from him. She is now dying in a
hospital bed, a "yellow shriveled mannequin." He
contrasts her present decay with "that body which
sprawled naked, gaping wide in shameless demand,
underneath Jim's naked body." For George, Doris is
"Bitch-Mother Nature," the female prerogative for
which the Church, the Law, and the State exist and
before which he is expected to bow and hide "his
unnatural head in shame." But George discovers
that he can no longer hate Doris. *"We are on the
same road,"* he muses, *"I shall follow you soon."*
While his hatred remained, he could find in her
something of Jim. Now he leaves her deathbed diminished. One more bit of Jim is lost.

In a more complicated way, George's extended
encounter with Charley also increases his aware-

ness of isolation. His relationship with her is based upon their common English background and their having shared each other's troubles. As intimate as their relationship is, each of them dependent on the other for support and comfort and the "magic" that allows them to pursue separate dreams while pretending they are identical, Charley is not content with being one of George's links to his past with Jim. She would like George to need her in a more personal, even sexual way.

As he leaves her house, tellingly located on Soledad Way, "she kisses him full on the mouth. And suddenly sticks her tongue right in . . . It's one of those drunken long shots which just might, at least theoretically, once in ten thousand tries, throw a relationship right out of its orbit and send it whizzing off on another." Like Doris, Charley is also "Bitch-Mother Nature." For all her sympathy and genuine love, she fails to accept or even to recognize a crucial dimension of the wholeness of George's personality.

George's alienation from even a friend like Charley is emphasized by his memory of the beach months of 1946, soon after he had met Jim: "The magic squalor of those hot nights, when the whole shore was alive with tongues of flame, the watch-fires of a vast naked barbarian tribe, each group or pair to itself and bothering no one, yet all a part of the life of the tribal encampment—swimming in the darkness, cooking fish, dancing to the radio, coupling without shame on the sand." More than a nostalgic reminiscence of youthful lust, this memory marks a new beginning for George.

This memory of a tribal past is a vision of community that is in pointed contrast to George's singleness. Embedded in it is an allusion to the "cloven tongues like as of fire" through which the

Holy Spirit appeared at Pentecost, symbolizing the
unity of mankind and the universality of God's offer
of grace (Acts 2:1-21). As a vision of community that
reconciles the conflicting needs of tribal acceptance
and individual assertion, this memory plays a vital
role in George's decision to embrace life and to
seek identity with others, while at the same time
preserving the integrity of his individuality.

George's actual decision to embrace life results
from the evening encounter with his student Kenny,
whom he had earlier told, "there are some things
you don't even *know* you know, until you're asked."
In his dialogue with Kenny, George suddenly becomes aware that *"what I know is what I am.* And I
can't tell you that. You have to find it out for yourself. I'm like a book you have to read. A book can't
read itself to you." George accepts himself here as
the total of his experiences.

This acceptance causes him to value not only
the past, but especially the present. He chides
Kenny: "Instead of trying to know, you commit the
inexcusable triviality of saying, 'he's a dirty old
man,' and turning this evening, which might be the
most unforgettable of your young life, into a
flirtation. . . . It's the enormous tragedy of everything nowadays: flirtation. Flirtation instead of
fucking, if you'll pardon my coarseness." If Kenny's
life is not transformed by the evening, George's is,
for he decides to fly to Mexico for Christmas, to
seize the present, to find love, to move beyond the
exile of his solitariness. Even the comic masturba-
tion scene, where he gradually progresses from
imagining others in sexual play to freely substitut-
ing himself for them, symbolizes his transformation
from passive observer to active participant.

Paradoxically, at least to Western minds,
George's decision to embrace life in the present, to

seek community, prepares him for death. Death, only suppositional in the novel, involves becoming part of a community larger than the gay minority or even the heterosexual majority. In death, George's spirit will merge with the universal consciousness, "that consciousness which is no one in particular, but which contains everyone and everything, past, present, and future, and extends unbroken beyond the uttermost stars."

Concerned as it is with decay and death, *A Single Man* has been described accurately as a *memento mori* sermon.[5] But it is more: the awareness of death heightens the need to live fully and to love. *A Single Man* is surely as much about living as about dying. It confronts the most vital issues of contemporary fiction and of modern life and offers in resolution to the problems of alienation and isolation a vision of community, of self-transcendence through universal consciousness and through involvement in the lives of others. In making concrete this resolution, the novel presents a sustained and moving portrait of male homosexual love—perhaps the most honest of such portraits in contemporary fiction—and plumbs insightfully and revealingly the homosexual plight, using homosexuality as a metaphor for alienation.

The vision of *A Single Man* is complex, even double: the assertions of individual uniqueness and of minority consciousness are regarded as indispensable worldly goals, but goals ultimately subsumed in the Vedantic idea of the oneness of life. All individuals are single in their separateness one from another, yet they are finally united in an oceanic consciousness. Thus, even as the novel charts George's growth from isolation toward worldly commitment, it also traces his emergence from the narrow confines of individual identity into an otherworldly union with the universal consciousness.

The novel's religious vision is stated most explicitly in an extended passage that uses rock pools and ocean as analogues for individual identity and impersonal universality:

Up the coast a few miles north, in a lava reef under the cliffs, there are a lot of rock pools. You can visit them when the tide is out. Each pool is separate and different, and you can, if you are fanciful, give them names. . . . Just as George and the others are thought of, for convenience, as individual entities, so you may think of a rock pool as an entity; though, of course, it is not. . . . The rocks of the pool hold their world together. And, throughout the day of the ebb tide, they know no other.

But that long day ends at last; yields to the nighttime of the flood. And, just as the waters of the ocean come flooding, darkening over the pools, so over George and the others in sleep come the waters of that other ocean. . . . We may surely suppose that, in the darkness of the full flood, some of these creatures are lifted from their pools to drift far out over the deep waters. But do they ever bring back, when the daytime of the ebb returns, any kind of catch with them? Can they tell us, in any manner, about their journey? Is there, indeed, anything for them to tell—except that the waters of the ocean are not really other than the waters of the pool?

In this passage, Isherwood distinguishes between the rock pools—the *Maya*, or mundane reality in which George exists as an individual person— and the ocean—the *Brahman*, or higher reality in which George is part of the universal consciousness. But the *Maya* is illusory and impermanent, and the differences isolating the individual rock pools are also illusory when measured in terms of the higher reality: "the waters of the ocean are not really other than the waters of the pool." Thus, for all George's fierce insistence on his individuality, the *Maya* of personal identity finally yields to the *Brahman* of impersonal universality, just as the waters of the rock pool are eventually merged with the waters of the ocean.

Significantly, George's escape from the narrow confines of the self constitutes religious as well as secular salvation. His metamorphosis from a prisoner of the past into a participant in the present is paralleled by a transformation from self-preoccupation to transcendent awareness. As with Paul in *Down There on a Visit*, George discovers "Truth, the unitive knowledge of the Godhead"—as Huxley defines the "purpose of human life"[6]—intuitively rather than discursively. He uses no specifically religious or Vedantic terminology, but he achieves a transfiguration of the spirit, first experiencing an epiphany in the ocean and then becoming in the course of his dialogue with Kenny "an oracular George, who may shortly begin to speak with tongues."

George's eventual arrival at spiritual truth is presaged early in the novel when he recognizes his reflection in the mirror as not "so much a face as the expression of a predicament. Here's what it has done to itself, here's the mess it has somehow managed to get itself into during its fifty-eight years." His visit to Doris magnifies his awareness that "*We are on the same road.*" Even his exultant pleasure in being numbered among "the ranks of that marvelous minority, The Living" and his enjoyment of the "easygoing physical democracy" of the gymnasium mark an increasing acceptance of his place in the human community. But George's spiritual awareness reaches its apogee in the sacramental "baptism of the surf" in which he and Kenny escape "across the border into the water-world."

In the ocean, George, "intent upon his own

rites of purification," gives himself wholly to the water: "he washes away thought, speech, mood, desire, whole selves, entire lifetimes; again and again he returns, becoming always cleaner, freer, less." He is suddenly swallowed by "a great, an apocalyptically great wave." He stands naked and tiny and unafraid in the mystery of the ocean's vastness, accepting the revelation of the wave's apocalypse.

Although George is unable to articulate the significance of this experience, he reveals its impact in his new courage and confidence. He comes to reject "dreary categories" that separate human beings. "I mean," he asks Kenny, "what is this life supposed to be *for*? Are we to spend it identifying each other with catalogues, like tourists in an art gallery? Or are we to try to exchange *some* kind of a signal, however garbled, before it's too late?" George's new interest in the meaning of life and in communicating that meaning is especially important in light of Huxley's remark that the degree to which one discovers on earth the unitive knowledge of the Godhead "determines the degree to which it will be enjoyed in the posthumous state."[7]

In the suppositional death that ends the novel, George is no longer a single man, in any of that term's many senses. His spirit escapes the confines of the rocks; it joins the "deep waters," unable any longer to associate with "what lies here, unsnoring on the bed . . . cousin to the garbage in the container on the back porch." In the nighttime of the flood, the waters of the pool merge with the waters of the ocean.

A Single Man is Isherwood's finest novel. Beautifully written in a style that alternates between poetic intensity and gentle irony, the book is a technical *tour de force* in which every nuance is perfectly controlled. Deftly combining a deeply felt minority consciousness and a transcendent religious vision, the novel brilliantly portrays its idiosyncratic, antiheroic hero as a type of Everyman with whom all readers can identify.

The book embodies what Alan Wilde describes as the lesson of Isherwood's career, "That as a writer becomes more religious he may also become more humanistic and more humane."[8] As Altman notes, "The bitterness/irony/amusement that go to make up the sensibility of the homosexual who moves continually between a gay and a straight world is perfectly caught in ... A *Single Man,* a book that is ... a much finer exploration of the homosexual sensibility than more touted works."[9] At the same time, however, the novel transcends the narrowness of any particular sensibility and explores a universal predicament. In understated prose tinged with humor, irony, and compassion, Isherwood not only captures the fullness of an individual life in a particular place at a specific time but also translates it into an emblem of the human condition in any place at any time.

8

~~~~~~

The Only Thing
That Really Matters:
A Meeting by the River

Set in a Hindu monastery on the banks of the Ganges near Calcutta, *A Meeting by the River* embodies most fully and most directly the religious and intellectual forces that have shaped all Isherwood's postwar fiction. Indeed, this latest of Isherwood's novels, published in 1967, even reinterprets such figures as the Truly Weak Man and the Evil Mother and such questions as the will to power and the efficacy of involvement that haunted his work before his conversion to Vedantism. In its fascinating account of two brothers, apparently polar opposites in temperament and belief, who finally reveal their essential similarity, the novel explores two convergent paths to the goal of self-knowledge and finds an ideal of brotherhood essential to both.

Isherwood has disclaimed any intention of making "final philosophical statements" in the novel, describing it as "an interplay of opposing attitudes and personalities."[1] By casting the book in the form of letters and diary entries, thus avoiding the use of a narrator altogether, he creates the illusion of impartiality in the comparison of the two brothers, one a worldly hedonist and the other an ascetic monk. In actuality, however, the book is not evenhanded at all: it affirms the Vedantic road to enlightenment. There is no question that the otherworldly brother experiences a rebirth of the spirit that distinguishes him from the amoral egoist whose conversion remains an ambiguous future possibility. Nevertheless, the vision that informs *A Meeting by the River* is nondogmatic. The path chosen by the less idealistic brother may also eventually lead him to the "safety and happiness" he desires.

The novel opens with Oliver's writing to his older brother, Patrick, asking him to inform their mother that he has entered a Hindu monastery and intends soon to take his final vows as a swami. Patrick agrees to his brother's request and asks permission to visit him in India on his journey east in connection with a film he is producing. Patrick arrives at the monastery intent on persuading Oliver to return to England. There ensue struggles both between the brothers and within each to justify their chosen ways of life. Patrick's perspective is expressed in letters he writes to their mother in Chapel Bridge; to his wife, Penelope, in London; and to his lover, Tom, in Los Angeles. Oliver's account of the struggles is recorded in his diary.

Although the brothers love each other, both nurse festering resentments and jealousies. Patrick resents their mother's favoritism toward his younger brother, and he feels threatened by Oliver's rejection of the worldly values that give his own life order and stability. Oliver has for a long time been in love with Patrick's wife, Penelope, and continues to be jealous of his brother. Seeing in Patrick all the worst manifestations of the ego he is striving to mortify, Oliver is fearful of his brother's continuing power over him.

For different reasons, both men subconsciously welcome the confrontation Patrick's visit to the monastery affords. Patrick plays a satanic role, tempting Oliver to abandon his new vocation by ever more refined inducements. The temptations culminate in a tacit offer of Penelope and an explicit exhortation to worldly power. Oliver views the temptations as embodiments of his own doubts, and he seizes Patrick's presence as an opportunity for rigorous self-examination. Less obviously, Patrick's role as tempter mirrors his dissatisfaction with his own life, and in the atmosphere of the monastery he is forced to question all his old verities.

A dream featuring his current infatuation, Tom, causes Patrick to consider a break with his family. A drunken telephone call from Tom to Patrick, mistakenly answered by Oliver, provokes an open but inconclusive confrontation between the two brothers. A dream in which Oliver feels the presence of Swami, his dead guru, finally convinces him of the genuineness of his commitment. Patrick ultimately reaffirms his allegiance to the all-forgiving and long-suffering Penelope and to their two daughters.

A Meeting by the River ends on a note of brotherly love. Oliver is inducted into the order, undergoing a ceremony symbolizing his death and rebirth. Patrick blesses his brother's decision, and the two men embrace. Significantly, however, neither changes the perspective in which he views the other. Patrick is convinced that Oliver will achieve worldly power as "the paleface prophet," and Oliver believes that Patrick is unknowingly in a state of grace.

The brothers who appear so different are actually very similar. As Oliver remarks, "Heredity has made us part of a single circuit, our wires are all connected." At one point, Patrick explains his relationship with Tom in crudely pornographic detail and then asks Oliver, "If you were in my shoes, what would you do? Or is being in my shoes too utterly unthinkable?" Oliver's reply, "It's perfectly thinkable . . . we're very much alike in some ways," is precisely correct. Although they are symbolic opposites—idealist and pragmatist, celibate and bisexual athlete, moralist and amoralist, saint and sinner—the brothers are both Truly Weak Men, insecure and self-doubting.

Ironically, each sees in the other his own worst fears, his own best fantasies. Oliver describes Patrick's power over him as "my own doubt and weakness," and thus the temptations Patrick poses are very real and genuinely attractive. But Oliver's idealism is similarly attractive to Patrick, whose own inchoate idealism is gradually exposed in the course of his stay at the monastery. Oliver's warning to his brother—"You'd better not get too interested [in religious questions]. It might be risky"—is well aimed, despite Patrick's profession of astonishment. Patrick's protest in his first letter to Oliver that "I am deeply interested [in your religious life], and on my own account quite as much as on yours" turns out to be far truer than either realizes. Moreover, both have a deep-seated need for genuine brotherhood, a fraternal union that includes spiritual as well as physical kinship.

The brothers are reminiscent of Michael and James Ransom of *The Ascent of F 6*, and their mother of Mrs. Ransom. As Patrick explains in the pivotal confrontation scene: "I'm afraid I must blame mother, entirely. . . . She cast her sons for roles in life, and they had to be different roles, of course, so that we shouldn't clash. I was to be the worldly success—that role was already taken before you appeared on the scene. So you were cast to be the unworldly one, the subtler, finer spirit who's above competition and shrinks from ambition in disgust as something vile and low. Poor old Olly!

You were born to play one part, but Mother cast you for another."

This explanation of the differences in the brothers' characters by the glib, psychologically oriented Patrick may or may not be valid. But his understanding of the will to power that underlies Oliver's humility, emphasized as well by his frequent comparisons of Oliver to Lawrence of Arabia, may unconsciously betray Patrick's repressed suspicion that his own worldliness is an ill-fitting role in which he was cast by an Evil Mother. Perhaps his true nature, the part he was born to play, is quite different from the role of worldly success in which his mother cast him.

That Patrick's wordly success and outward conformity are largely attributable to a need to please his mother is evident from his letters to her. His complaint to Oliver that their mother prefers her younger son—"She *lives* for you. And therefore only you have the power to hurt her"—is deeply revealing, particularly since Patrick consistently portrays himself as a martyr who sacrifices his happiness to please her and Oliver as a selfishly motivated free spirit who pleases only himself. In one letter, Patrick tells his mother, "I know . . . that you've grieved because Olly has never found himself a partner in life and never given you grandchildren," and then pointedly adds, "Penny and I have done our best to fill *that* gap, haven't we?" In another letter, he describes Oliver as one "who always seems to do exactly what he wants to do, not what he has to do." Patrick then remarks: "I do find that most inspiring—though what would happen to the world if we all followed Oliver's example, I tremble to think! Nearly all of us are the slaves of our obligations, however willingly we may fulfil them."

In fact, however, Patrick performs his obligations much less willingly than he pretends, for he is always conscious of an important distinction between duty and happiness. Self-described as an arrested teenager, Patrick regards his marriage primarily as a duty and his wife as a surrogate mother who enforces his adherence to a conformity at odds with his happiness. He tells the allusively named Penelope, who waits patiently at home while, Ulysses-like, he pursues adventures abroad, "You know how absolutely I rely on your strength," and he complacently admits to being the weaker half of the couple.

The relationship with Tom begins as just another in a long series of adolescent flings in which Patrick runs from his obligations, "looking for my teen-age self and flexing my muscles." But at the monastery he has a vision, "actually a glimpse of a life which [Tom] and I were living together. . . . this life I got a glimpse of was of such a closeness as I'd never even imagined could exist between two human beings, because it was a life *entirely without fear*." As it turns out, however, Patrick finally rejects this prospect of happiness in favor of the "safety and freedom" represented by the maternal Penelope. Significantly, though, the values of trust and closeness first made manifest in the dream prompted by Tom are ultimately recognized by Patrick as essential to his future life with Penelope.

A Meeting by the River never makes explicit the exact basis of Patrick's rejection of a life "in which two men learn to trust each other so completely that there's no fear left and they experience and share everything together in the flesh and in the spirit." Tom's drunken telephone call is crucial to the decision, but exactly how it is crucial remains speculative, particularly since Patrick is repeatedly exposed as an accomplished liar whose word can never be accepted at facc value.

It may be that in the discussion following the telephone call, Oliver's blunt advice that if Penelope and the children "only represent duty to you, . . . you ought to leave them," shocks Patrick into a reassessment of his relationships. He may indeed be sincere in his statement that "duty often seems to me to be the only thing one can really count on, in the long run. Happiness may be thrown in as an occasional bonus, but one never knows how long it will last." It may be that Tom's drunken behavior simply convinces Patrick that the young man is too immature to be the partner in the union of flesh and spirit he envisioned. Patrick may be honest in his confession to Tom that "I begin to see our relationship in an altogether different light, and for the first time I feel guilty about it, because now I see that I involved you in something which was far out of your depth." But in either case, Patrick's decision is also motivated by the cowardice that is an integral aspect of his conformity.

Patrick's ugly letter to Tom breaking off their relationship constitutes a shameful retreat into the insecurity and conformity that have characterized his entire life. Although Patrick had earlier explained the Hindu indifference to homosexuality, in the letter to Tom he brazenly lies about the effect of the telephone conversation on Oliver's position in the monastery, pretending to a concern that his brother might "punish himself . . . with severe self-inflicted penances" for not telling the "unvarnished truth" to his fellow monks.

Earlier Patrick had bravely declared his intention to "face other people without fear and let them see us as we are"; but in the final letter to Tom, he condemns the young man's honesty in defying so-

cial conventions. Fresh from his visionary experience, Patrick had doubted whether the intense
closeness of an ideal homosexual relationship "is
possible between a man and a woman," but in the
final letter he implies that "out-and-out homosexuals" are "somewhat wilful freaks" and advises
Tom to attempt a relationship with a woman. Unconsciously revealing his insecurity, Patrick cyni-
cally adds: "Being married does make a lot of things
easier, because the world accepts marriage at its
face value, without asking what goes on behind the
scenes—whereas it's always a bit suspicious of
bachelors!"

For all the changes wrought by his stay at the
monastery, Patrick remains a mother-fixated coward
who fears open nonconformity as a threat to his fragile system of values. He remains a little boy who
plays at the games of being a husband and a father
and who relies on Penelope to protect him from the
consequences of his cruel irresponsibility. If Tom
somehow manages to get in touch with her, he tells
Penelope, "I'm sure you'll know how to cope with
him. I shall never forget how understanding but
firm you were with that poor tiresome child from
Stockholm. (You see, I've even forgotten his
name!)"

Although outwardly charming, Patrick is
among the most unpleasant characters in all of
Isherwood's fiction. A Truly Weak Man, he is reminiscent of Philip Lindsay in *All the Conspirators.*
There may, however, be hope for Patrick. His repressed vision of a life without fear may signal at
least the possibility of an eventual maturity for the
middle-aged adolescent. His dissatisfaction with
his life may be an unconscious recognition of the
pain of hunger beneath everything that may ultimately propel him toward salvation.

If Patrick is mother-fixated, then Oliver, on the other hand, "is a son in search of an ideal father."[2] His search has led him to embrace and then to reject a half-dozen prophets whose feet proved to be of clay. As Patrick writes Penelope, "Not one of them lasted long. Olly softened them up with his desperate will-to-believe and then mercilessly poked them to pieces with his doubts." But Oliver's allegiance to his guru survives the tests of fear and doubt; and by the end of the novel he is convinced that although Swami is dead, "nevertheless he was now with me—*and that he is with me always, wherever I am.*"

Isherwood's depiction of Swami is an advance over the earlier portrayals of such saints as Sarah in *The World in the Evening* and Augustus Parr in *Down There on a Visit.* "Something about him fascinated me, from the first moment," Oliver writes, "it was his quiet unemphatic air of assurance." Swami, "just by being what he was, intrigued and mystified me and undermined my basic assumptions as no one else had ever done before." Eventually, Oliver moved in with Swami and functioned as his son, a role that was awkward at first, he tells Patrick, because "Father died when we were both so young." He became the Swami's disciple "in the literal Hindu monastic sense, a novice monk who serves his guru and is trained by him like a son, and who will become a swami himself in due course."

The action of *A Meeting by the River* largely centers around Oliver's internal struggle to prepare himself for the final monastic vows, to mortify his vicious "monkey-face" ego so that he can die to the world and be reborn in the spirit. He passes the series of escalating tests, from Patrick's exhibitionistic temptation of the flesh, in which Oliver "couldn't help being aware of [Patrick's] rather big penis slap-

ping against his bare thigh" as he exercises nude, to
the "appallingly attractive" temptation of worldly
power used for humanitarian ends. Central to
Oliver's final resolve to remain at the monastery is
his vision of Swami.

Structurally, the vision is parallel to Patrick's
dream of a union of flesh and spirit with Tom.
Oliver's vision resolves his lingering doubts about
the efficacy of involvement in the world and expresses his genuine need to achieve union with his
Swami and with his brother, a union that renders all
the sibling rivalries and jealousies irrelevant and
that constitutes an escape from the confines of the
ego. In the dream, "We were domestically together
as we used to be in the old days. Swami was sitting
cross-legged on a bed or couch—the room was non-
descript and not recognizable—and I was making
tea for him, boiling water in a kettle on a gas-ring. I
felt happy and at peace, as I always used to be while
doing him any small service."

Oliver explains the tea-making as a symbolic
act: "The spiritual significance was all that ultimately mattered, and it was the same in either case.
In other words, I really and deeply understood, at
long last, what Swami used to keep trying to teach
me and what I used to repeat after him so glibly
without any true understanding, about the symbolic
nature of all action." Thus, the vision provides Oliver an intuitive knowledge of the value of nonattached action.

The dream is also a vision of union, "the one
and only thing that really matters," as Oliver had
earlier described his feeling of oneness with the
other monks preparing for the final vows, a feeling
that transcends all the many differences between
himself and them. In the dream in which he senses
the presence of Swami, he knows that "we are

never separated." Moreover, the vision also unites him with Patrick, for "now it seemed to me that Patrick was very close to us—in the next room, as it were. And I was aware that he was an established part of our life, the three of us belonged together intimately and I accepted this as a matter of course."

The need for fraternal union is one that both brothers share. When Patrick declares his love to Tom, he remarks, "since I had that dream, I'm certain that *you* could be my brother—the kind of brother I now know I've been searching for all these years, without ever quite daring to admit to myself what it was that I wanted." By the end of the novel, he, like Oliver, feels united with his real brother, in this case as part of a trinity that includes Penelope. In his final letter to her, Patrick writes, "however far His Holiness may choose to withdraw himself from *me*, I don't care, I feel so close to *him* tonight! . . . I mean, I feel such closeness in the thought of us three together. Each one of us will belong to the other two always, even if we never set eyes on Olly again."

Brotherhood, both natural and symbolic, is finally revealed as the "only thing that really matters" in *A Meeting by the River*. The union of the two natural brothers at the end of the novel is the culmination of their long searches for symbolic brotherhood, quests that have led one to the glimpse of a Whitmanesque ideal of homosexual love and the other to the achievement of spiritual brotherhood in a monastery. After Oliver completes the final ceremony of *sannyas*, all trace of the foreignness that separated him from his brother monks vanishes: "for the first time, there were no barriers between us, I wasn't an alien." With characteristic panache, Patrick greets him by dropping to his knees and bowing down before him. The two exchange a kiss, and all the onlookers agree "how very right and proper it was that we two brothers should love each other."

The novel's happy ending—with one brother firmly committed to a religious vocation and the other to a new relationship with his neglected wife and both men happily accepting each other—is a measure of the changes wrought by the brothers' meeting by the river. The two are not equally happy, however, and they have achieved quite different levels of self-knowledge.

Patrick's self-proclaimed happiness is deeply suspect, based as it is on deception and on a cowardly denial of the vision he receives at the monastery. Oliver's, on the other hand, is genuine, achieved through scrupulous honesty and by an adherence to his vision. Despite these essential differences, both brothers acknowledge the metamorphosing power of their encounter, though they interpret the changes they perceive in different terms. The worldly Patrick sees them as psychological responses and the unworldly Oliver as religious transformations. The novel allows the interpretations to coexist, but strongly endorses Oliver's version.

That the religious view dominates is indicated by the fact that both brothers separately acknowledge a supernatural influence. Oliver's repeated conviction that nothing in life is accidental may be expected from someone in a religious vocation. More telling are the frequent observations by Patrick that testify to a pervasive otherworldly presence. In one letter to Penelope, after roundly condemning "the peculiar hypnotic power of this place and its way of life, or rather anti-life," he admits, "Still, I do have the uncanniest feeling that this situation is drifting out of my hands, that I'm not quite

in control of my own actions, even." In his final letter to his wife, he pays tribute to the salutary effects
of the monastery: "Whatever may be said against
this place—and I *have* said a good deal, haven't I—
it does seem to create an atmosphere in which you
can think your own thoughts more objectively and
indeed almost look at them while you're thinking
them."

These grudging admissions from Patrick, cou-
pled with his acknowledgment of the sincerity of
the monks, "so wise in their own kind of wisdom
and so childlike in ours," tend to validate the Vedantic position. They also function rhetorically to
support Oliver's belief that Patrick is unknowingly
in a state of grace. Oliver interprets Patrick's dissatisfaction with his life as "the first faint beginning of
an awareness that some new and unknown power is
working inside him." "If you look at this objectively," Oliver remarks, "it's a pretty comic situation. Poor old Paddy—he's in a state of grace! And
he's going to discover it the hard way. He doesn't
dream what he's in for, but he'll find out before
long."

A Meeting by the River is, thus, a comic novel
incorporating "the Divine play of Maya."[3] From this
perspective, Patrick is indeed the "very sick patient" attended by the gravely concerned yet
amused Swami of Oliver's vision, "shaking his head
over Patrick, so to speak, with an air of indulgent
amusement, as if to say, 'Oh my goodness, what *will*
he be up to next?'" Fittingly, even the union of
brotherhood that concludes the book is described as
part of a "tremendous joke." Both brothers nearly
convulse with laughter. Patrick whispers, "Well
Olly, you've *really* gone and torn it now!" and Oliver replies, "Looks like I'm stuck with it, doesn't
it?"

A *Meeting by the River* is among Isherwood's most intriguing novels. A powerful study of brothers different in personality and style, it finally reveals the commonality within them and offers the concept of brotherhood itself as a means of escaping the imprisoning ego. Although it eschews the subtle and evocative prose of *A Single Man*, *A Meeting by the River* gains surprising stylistic variety by juxtaposing the extravagant flourishes of Patrick's letters with the spare flatness of Oliver's diary entries, using the divergent styles as signatures revealing of personality. Like *The Memorial*, Isherwood's latest novel masterfully exploits the power of reticence, forcing the reader to participate actively in evaluating the experiences of the two brothers. And by creating an illusion of impartiality in the conflict between Oliver and Patrick, Isherwood nondogmatically affirms the Vedantic vision of universal brotherhood.

9

~~~~~~

Glimpses of Inner Truth:
Biography and Autobiography

In concluding his most recent book, *My Guru and His Disciple,* published in 1980, the seventy-five-year-old Isherwood remarks on "the enduring fascination of my efforts to describe my life-experience in my writing" and on his "interest in the various predicaments of my fellow-travellers on this journey" through life. This fascination and this interest are embodied in the novels on which his reputation rests, but they are expressed most directly in his nonfictional works, among which are numbered five remarkable books that illuminate his life and times. Although written independently of each other, four of these books may be regarded as installments in a multivolume autobiography, each presenting a different slice of the writer's life; and the fifth is a travel book that is most interesting when it is most revealing of its author.

The nonfiction books are particularly valuable for the light they cast on the novels. The autobiographical works explain the personal myths Isherwood created for himself and the artistic, intellectual, sexual, and spiritual values that the novels incorporate. Since the novels are themselves autobiographical at base—art distilled from life—the nonfictional autobiographies also aid in charting the fine distinctions between art and life that are central to the artistry of the novels, distinctions inevitably problematic in the work of a writer whose greatest gifts are those of ironic observation and introspection rather than of invention.

But even in the nonfiction books, Isherwood characteristically blurs the conventional boundaries separating fiction and actuality. "Read it as a novel," he advises in the preface to his early autobiography, *Lions and Shadows*. The injunction is equally applicable to the ostensible biography of his parents, *Kathleen and Frank*, and to his account of his life during the 1930s told from the perspective of the 1970s, *Christopher and His Kind*.

The nonfiction books, artfully designed to be read as novels, present experience filtered through the gauze of a revisionist personality. Written with piercing insight in a masterly style remarkable for its clarity and resonance, they are the work of a consummate artist intent on recording realities that may be only coincidentally similar to the actual experiences of the author. Although the books are unsparingly honest, they may not always be literally accurate. But in different ways each offers "glimpses of inner truth," as Isherwood describes the goal of *My Guru and His Disciple*.

Lions and Shadows

Published in 1938, *Lions and Shadows* is Isherwood's portrait of the artist as a young man. An absorbing account of the frustrations of a precocious but immature writer, it is subtitled "An Education in the Twenties." It traces the life of the young novelist from his public school days following the Great War through his inglorious stint at Cambridge as a rebellious undergraduate and in London as a half-hearted medical student to his departure from England for Berlin on March 14, 1929. The education it traces is the growth of a Truly Weak Man who strikes a Byronic pose as "Isherwood the Artist" into the mature, self-exiled author who—some eight years after the last event recounted in the book—observes with scientific detachment his earlier self as an exhibit "in the vast freak museum of our neurotic generation."

The novelistic structure of the book is essentially a series of rejections and failures: rejection of old school loyalties, of academic pursuits, of conventional heroism, of aestheticism, and finally, of England itself; and failure at Cambridge, in medical school, in personal relationships, and as a novelist. Paradoxically, however, this series of rejections and failures leads to a dissatisfaction that contains within it the possibility of self-acceptance and artistic success, the possibility of maturity. "Did I really want to sham my way through life, impressing other people, perhaps, but knowing myself for a coward, at heart?" the young Isherwood asks himself in a crucial passage that looks forward to an emergent maturity. The repeated failures of education in the 1920s finally culminate in the realization, "As long as I remained a sham, my writing would be sham, too."

That the young Isherwood finally attains maturity is evidenced by the existence of the book itself—a work that is clearly not sham. But *Lions and Shadows* does not detail exactly how the young protagonist metamorphoses into the accomplished, self-knowing author, except to imply that the change of scene from London to Berlin is largely responsible. Thus, the book's greatest success is as an indictment of middle-class English life in the 1920s rather than as an account of a novelist's education.

Although the book is narrated in the first person, it is curiously impersonal. "A young man living

at a certain period in a certain European country,"
Isherwood writes in his prefatory note, "is sub-
jected to a certain kind of environment, certain
stimuli, certain influences. That the young man
happens to be myself is only of secondary importance." *Lions and Shadows* is, thus, not "in the ordi-
nary journalistic sense of the word, an autobiography; it contains no 'revelations'; it is never 'indis-
creet'; it is not even entirely 'true.'" The objectivity with which the narrator observes his younger self functions to transform the Truly Weak Man
into a representative of an entire generation of
young artists and writers alienated from their society, haunted by a "tireless Sense of Guilt," and
struggling toward maturity in an age dominated by
hypocrisy and snobbery.

In order to make his earlier self a representative figure of his generation, Isherwood both distorts and suppresses aspects of his life in the 1920s.
He suppresses references to his relationship with
his mother, the most important person in his life
during this period; and he fails to mention his sexual heterodoxy, although his very reticence in discussing his sex life might itself have signaled his
homosexuality to sophisticated readers in the late
1930s. Even in the candid discussions of war and
The Test—"We young writers of the middle 'twenties were all suffering, more or less subconsciously,
from a feeling of shame that we hadn't been old
enough to take part in the European war"—he fails
to reveal the death of his hero-father in that war, the
particular death that made The Test so urgent for
him and that engendered his own irrational guilt.

He also distorts his autobiography by presenting himself as far more passive and submissive than
he really was. Whereas Isherwood was actually the
dominant figure among his circle of friends in the
1920s, in *Lions and Shadows* he is depicted as a

follower rather than a leader. He imitates others in concocting escapist fantasies, in creating a "school-saga world," in studying medicine, in embracing the philosophy of Homer Lane, in abandoning England for Berlin.

Although the Evil Mother is conspicuously absent save for cryptic references to "my female relative" (and perhaps the conspicuousness of her absence constitutes a presence), the world of *Lions and Shadows* is the world of *All the Conspirators* and *The Memorial*. It is inhabited by Isherwood's closest friends, thinly disguised with fictitious names and caricatured with a novelist's license. These caricatures mirror various aspects of the young Isherwood's own neurotic insecurity, thus contributing to the broad scope of the book's indictment of English values. But insofar as these friends—Allen Chalmers (Edward Upward), Hugh Weston (W. H. Auden), Stephen Savage (Stephen Spender), and Philip Linsley (Hector Wintle)—were themselves destined to become important figures in the literary world of the 1930s, their portraits give *Lions and Shadows* an interest quite apart from their thematic function in underlining the deadening influence of English society in the 1920s.

These portraits are remarkably vivid. They are sketched with a caricaturist's deft exaggeration but deepened by an ironist's shrewd insight. For instance, this snapshot of Spender economically captures the awkwardness and vitality of an intense youth by exaggerating his clumsiness and incongruously—yet convincingly—comparing him with wild flowers: "He burst in upon us, blushing, sniggering loudly, contriving to trip over the edge of the carpet—an immensely tall, shambling boy of nineteen, with a great scarlet poppy-face, wild frizzy hair, and eyes the violent color of bluebells."

The caricatures of Auden are especially memorable. They isolate vivid details such as his "great flaps of ears" and "his narrow scowling pudding-white face," and they use casual wit to evoke deep feeling. This portrait of Auden as an untidy young poet is marvelously comic, yet drawn with great affection:

He could never resist the sight of a piano, no matter whether it was in the refreshment room of a German railway station or the drawing room of a strange house: down he would sit, without so much as taking off his hat, and begin to play his beloved hymn tunes, psalms and chants—the last remnants of his Anglican upbringing. When he had finished the keyboard would be littered with ash and tobacco from his huge volcano-like pipe. He smoked enormously, insatiably: "Insufficient weaning," he explained. "I must have something to *suck*." And he drank more cups of tea per day than anybody else I have ever known. It was as if his large, white, apparently bloodless body needed continual reinforcements of warmth.

The fullest portrait in *Lions and Shadows* is of Edward Upward, Isherwood's closest friend during the 1920s. At Cambridge, the two form an alliance against the "poshocracy," the highest social circle of the college, and they collaborate in the construction of an elaborate fantasy world. The bizarre, surrealistic Mortmere fantasies represent an attempt to escape the hypocritical conformity of English society in general and of Cambridge in particular. Isherwood later described the alternative world of Mortmere as "a sort of anarchist paradise in which all accepted moral and social values were turned upside down and inside out, and every kind of extravagant behavior was possible and usual."[1]

But in *Lions and Shadows*, the young Isherwood finally concludes that "Mortmere seemed to have brought us to a dead end. The cult of romantic strangeness, we both knew, was a luxury for the comfortable University fireside; it could not save you from the drab realities of cheap lodgings and a dull, underpaid job." Upward eventually finds in Marxism the "formula which would transform our private fantasies and amusing freaks and bogies into valid symbols of the ills of society and the toils and aspirations of our daily lives." The young Isherwood rejects the rebellious escapism of Mortmere—"I wanted to stop playing the rebel myself. I wanted to be absorbed in the crowd"—and departs for Berlin to begin "yet another stage of my journey" toward maturity.

Lions and Shadows is both a powerful account of a young man's struggle to discover his authentic self and an affecting anatomy of a disinherited generation. Presenting himself as "the neurotic hero, the Truly Weak Man," Isherwood exposes the insecurity, ignorance, and fear of the generation that matured after the Great War. He resolves his personal dilemma by escaping England and by developing in Berlin his own distinctive style as the ironic observer. Asserting the dictum "The style is the man," he implies that in self-discovery lies artistic truth as well as personal fulfillment.

The Condor and the Cows

The Condor and the Cows is the travel diary of a six-month-long trip to South America that Isherwood and his friend William Caskey began in September 1947. Published in 1949, the book is illustrated with superb photographs by Caskey. While working on *The Condor and the Cows*, Isherwood wrote to John Lehmann: "I am churning out a travel-book, which is going to be my longest and worst book, I fear. I just can't do straight journalism, and the truth is that South America *bored* me, and I am ashamed that it bored me, and I hate it for making me feel ashamed."[2] Despite these fears, however, the completed book is altogether successful, and Isherwood later came to view it as "one of my best books."[3]

The title indicates the two distinct geographical areas that the trip encompassed: the condor as the symbol of the Andean mountain states, and the cows as the symbol of the Argentine. Isherwood enlivens his account of the journey from Venezuela to Colombia to Ecuador to Peru to Bolivia and, finally, to Argentina with quick character sketches of fellow tourists, oil field workers, missionaries, and figures from the arenas of literature, art, and politics. In addition, he enriches the travel diary with brief reflections on subjects as diverse as penal reform, racial prejudice, the role of the Catholic Church in South America, and his own status as an Anglo-American.

One reviewer justly complained that *The Condor and the Cows* suffers as a travel book because Isherwood is "oddly insensitive to landscape" and comes to life only when his gifts as a storyteller can be used.[4] Yet the great virtue of the book is that it is so atypical of its genre in being so personal. This subjectivity is perhaps best illustrated in Isherwood's reaction to the ancient Peruvian city of Cuzco. "There is no sense in my trying to describe Cuzco," he confesses, "I should only be quoting from the guide-book." But what follows this disclaimer is a personal response worth far more than any imaginable descriptions of the scene in a conventional travel book: "What remains with you is the sense of a great outrage, magnificent but unforgivable. The Spaniards tore down the Inca temples and grafted splendid churches and mansions to their foundations. This is one of the most beautiful monuments to bigotry and sheer stupid brutality in the whole world."

The book is extraordinarily well written, and it
is informed by a liberal humanism reminiscent of E.
M. Forster. A shrewd observer of the explosive
South American political climate, Isherwood is neither sentimental nor cynical. Always conscious of
the enormous amount of human suffering about
him, he is neither condescending nor solemn. Indeed, he frequently combines seriousness and humor, as when he comments of the Incas: "They
were certainly an impressive people. But they fill
me, personally, with a kind of horror. I find them, as
we used to say during the Evelyn Waugh period,
madly ungay."

The Condor and the Cows bears witness to
Isherwood's interest in religion at this stage of his
life. "Even if you discount fifty per cent of all criticism," he observes, "it can't be denied that the
Church in South America is a disgrace to Catholicism." He also berates "the militant atheists of the
Left Wing": "It is all very well to brand certain cults
and legends as superstitious, and to attack the political crimes of the historic sects, but have they never
stopped to ask themselves what religion is *for*?
How in the world do they imagine they can make
their free democratic community function when
they have removed the whole spiritual basis of con-
sent?"

When he visits the Ramakrishna Mission in a
suburb of Buenos Aires, Isherwood notes that
"Hindus aren't constrained by that unfortunate
Western notion that serious subjects must necessarily be taken seriously; they don't confuse laughter
with levity. Ramakrishna's own spiritual genius was
frequently expressed in humour—not the sly clever
kind, but real rampageous clowning, childlike silli-
ness, extravagance worthy of the Marx Brothers."
Isherwood's emphasis on the importance of fun as a
by-product of spirituality is deeply revealing of his

own religious commitment: "It is utterly subversive, outrageous, unself-conscious, improper, infectious. Indeed, it is one of the purest and most beautiful aspects of love."

Isherwood's comments on subjects as diverse as Evita Perón and Lawrence of Arabia may be offered as final evidence of the unexpected treasures in *The Condor and the Cows*. After condemning Evita Perón's opponents for attacking her allegedly lurid past and her humble origin—"This is not only uncharitable and snobbish; it is politically idiotic"—Isherwood remarks: "Señora Perón's past is the most sympathetic thing about her; and her critics would do much better to concentrate on her present and her future. . . . She may have been a bad actress once, but today she is a highly efficient demagogue." Of T. E. Lawrence, he comments: "He is a part of the mess I am in. What bind me to him are his faults—his instability, his masochism, his insane inverted pride."

The Condor and the Cows is an absorbing book, consistently entertaining and frequently revealing. If it is not wholly successful as a travel book, it nevertheless offers many other compensations, particularly those of humane intelligence and shrewd observation. The book even features the reunion of Herr Issyvoo with a fellow denizen of 1930s Berlin, Berthold Szczesny ("Bubi" in *Christopher and His Kind*), now a successful businessman in Buenos Aires, who salutes his friend with a commissioned poem celebrating the old days in the Cosy Corner bar. *The Condor and the Cows* is, as Brian Finney describes it, "a monument to Isherwood's professionalism as a writer."[5] Moreover, in its measured informality and warmth, it is also a thoroughly human document that enriches the Isherwood canon.

Kathleen and Frank

Subtitled "The Autobiography of a Family,"
Kathleen and Frank is a remarkable social history
as well as an intriguing investigation into the ori-
gins of Isherwood's personal mythology. Published
in 1971, the book consists principally of letters from
his father to his mother and of selections from his
mother's diaries, supplemented by Isherwood's
own comments on his family history. Writing from
the perspective of a sixty-seven-year-old man,
Isherwood refers to his parents and to his earlier
self by their Christian names and in the third person. He functions as a kind of impersonal editor
who fills in the gaps in the unfolding story and who
clarifies the context with historical information and
insightful speculation.

At the same time, however, the narrator is increasingly aware of a continuity of consciousness
that links him not only to his earlier self but to his
mother and father as well. He finally acknowledges
that "heredity and kinship create a woven fabric. . . . Impossible to say exactly where Kathleen
and Frank end and Richard and Christopher begin;
they merge into each other." This insight, similar to
Oliver's perception about his relationship to Patrick
in *A Meeting by the River*—"Heredity has made us
part of a single circuit, our wires are all connected"—constitutes a dominant theme in the
book. *Kathleen and Frank* thus becomes a project
of self-discovery as well as a belated tribute to the
author's parents. Ostensibly a biography of them, it
proves to be "chiefly about Christopher."

The center of the narrative is the romance of
Kathleen and Frank, whose long and troubled
courtship culminated in their marriage in 1903. An
artist and a soldier, Frank Bradshaw-Isherwood was
a member of a distinguished Cheshire family whose

ancestors included John Bradshaw, the judge who presided over the trial that condemned Charles I to death in 1649, and whose holdings included Marple Hall, a large Elizabethan country house, and Wyberslegh Hall, a lesser seat where Isherwood was born in 1904. Kathleen was the daughter of Frederick Machell-Smith, a prosperous wine merchant, and his wife, Emily Greene, a beautiful but restless woman, an avid theatergoer and "a great psychosomatic virtuoso who could produce high fevers, large swellings and mysterious rashes within the hour; her ailments were roles into which she threw herself with abandon."

Although the Bradshaw-Isherwoods were more socially prominent than the Machell-Smiths, Frederick vigorously opposed the match, ostensibly because as a second son and a soldier Frank could not afford to support Kathleen adequately. Emily, on the other hand, allied herself with the lovers, perhaps in recognition of her husband's approaching death and her psychological dependence on her daughter. The courtship of Kathleen and Frank, marked as it was by unseemly haggling over the marriage settlement by the families of both partners, reads like a Victorian social comedy. But the story includes moments of tenderness and playfulness as well. For all their lack of experience and the limitations of their class, Kathleen and Frank were both capable of genuine feeling.

Isherwood's parents are fascinating for two reasons. The first is their inherent interest as individual human beings, and the second their unwitting function as representatives of their class and their period. Although W. H. Auden complained of Kathleen that "her remarks are too typical of her class to be considered her own,"[6] she actually embodies her era's conventional attitudes in a highly individualized fashion. Her sense of duty, her inhibitions, her class consciousness, her mindless patriotism, her instinctive conservatism all mirror the middle-class values of late Victorian and Edwardian England, but in a revealingly personal way. The very narrowness of her perspective gives Kathleen's diary importance as a social document that exposes in concrete terms the personal impact of such public events as the deaths of Queen Victoria and King Edward VII, the Boer War, the Irish troubles, and the Great War. Moreover, her penchant for the romantic and the dramatic gives her limited point of view sustained interest. As Isherwood notes, "She saw her own life as History and its anniversaries as rites to be celebrated. She could invest minor domestic events with an epic quality."

Kathleen dominates the book, but Frank is actually the more interesting individual, for he is a more subtle and less predictable type. An amateur artist and musician, he warned Kathleen that "I am not manly, I like to be wooed. . . . I believe you know that I shall make a much better husband than lover." He did in fact make a very good husband, and more surprisingly, a good officer as well. He was also an excellent father. In letters written from France shortly before he was killed in battle in May of 1915, he reveals an endearing respect for his elder son's nonconformity. Observing that the point of sending Christopher to boarding school was to "flatten him out, so to speak, and to make him like other boys," he remarks: "When all is said and done, I don't know that it is at all desirable or necessary, and I for one would much rather have him as he is." In another letter he writes: "I don't think it matters very much what Christopher learns as long as he remains himself and keeps his individuality and develops on his own lines."

His death on the battlefield transformed Frank into a Hero-Father, Kathleen into a Holy Widow-

Mother, and Christopher into a Sacred Orphan. Much of Isherwood's life can be explained in terms of his rebellion against these mythopoeic roles. In defiance of The Others, who cast Frank as a Hero-Father, Christopher selected certain of Frank's characteristics and censored others in order to translate him into a father figure of his own devising, the Anti-Heroic Hero. "The Anti-Heroic Hero always appears in uniform," Christopher explains, "because this is his disguise; he isn't really a soldier. He is an artist who has renounced his painting, music and writing in order to dedicate his life to an antimilitary masquerade. He lives this masquerade right through, day by day to the end, and crowns his own performance by actually getting himself killed in battle."

Adopting a self-created role of Anti-Son, Christopher dedicated himself to scorning Kathleen's role of Holy Widow-Mother. He used her as "an opponent to prod him continually into revolt." She became the counterforce that gave him strength in his rebellion against English respectability. But their opposition was intimate, and she always remained a member of his private audience: "One of the aims of his writing—never quite achieved—was to seduce her into liking it in spite of herself." Through her opposition to Christopher, Kathleen "more than anybody else ... saved him from becoming a mother's boy, a churchgoer, an academic, a conservative, a patriot and a respectable citizen." His decision to settle permanently in the United States, "thus separating himself from Mother and Motherland at one stroke," was both a ritual act of breaking free from her and the termination of his opposition to her.

In the book's final pages, as he looks back on his relationship with his mother from the vantage point of his own advancing age, Isherwood is struck

by the irony of how closely his development in the
United States paralleled her hopes for him: "By
teaching in colleges he had become an academic,
even if he had also become a clown. By embracing
Vedanta he had joined the ranks of the religious,
even while remaining anti-church. By opposing
those fellow-citizens whom he regarded as a menace to his adopted country he had turned into a patriot, even though his enemies did all the flag-wav-
ing." Even his diary keeping, his ability to impart
an epic quality to minor domestic events, and his
penchant for constructing countermyths link him
with her.

A compelling and candid book that is at once
social history, biography, and autobiography,
Kathleen and Frank is also a lovely token of recon-
ciliation between a rebellious son and his conventional parents. More than that, it is a demonstration
that the search for oneself necessarily involves the
search for others. In *Kathleen and Frank*, Christopher's search for himself leads to his discovery of
his parents, which in turn yields a more profound
self-discovery than he could possibly have anticipated when he began reading through Kathleen's
diaries and Frank's letters. He finally understands
that "if these diaries and letters were part of his project, he was part of theirs—for they in themselves
were a project, too." Fittingly, the book ends with a
benediction: "So now Christopher's project has become theirs; their demand to be recorded is met by
his eagerness to record. For once the Anti-Son is in
perfect harmony with his Parents, for he can say,
'Our will be done!'"

Christopher and His Kind, 1929-1939

"To Christopher, Berlin meant Boys," observes

Isherwood in his 1976 reassessment of the decade
for which he is most famous, the 1930s. At the very
beginning of *Christopher and His Kind*, he announces that "the book I am now going to write will
be as frank and factual as I can make it, especially as
far as I myself am concerned. It will therefore be a
different kind of book from *Lions and Shadows* and
not, strictly speaking, a sequel to it. However, I
shall begin at the point where the earlier book ends:
twenty-four-year-old Christopher's departure from
England on March 14, 1929, to visit Berlin for the
first time in his life." The book concludes ten years
later with the emigration of Isherwood and Auden
to the United States.

A revisionist reinterpretation of a legendary
era, *Christopher and His Kind* is a sexual and political autobiography. Central to the book is the homosexuality that had to be suppressed in the author's
earlier fictional and nonfictional accounts of the
period. "At school," Isherwood writes, "Christopher had fallen in love with many boys and been
yearningly romantic about them. At college he had
at last managed to get into bed with one. This was
due entirely to the initiative of his partner, who,
when Christopher became scared and started to
raise objections, locked the door, and sat down
firmly on Christopher's lap." Setting the keynote for
this brave and defiant book, Isherwood adds: "I am
still grateful to him." And he explains that his first
visit to Berlin—"one of the decisive events of my
life"—was motivated by a need to escape the social
and sexual restrictions of life in England: "to be infatuated was what he had come to Berlin for."

Christopher and His Kind makes clear that homosexuality has been one of the central aspects of
Isherwood's life and that the homophobia of Western society necessarily invested his sexuality with
political significance. "Girls are what the state and

the church and the law and the press and the medical profession endorse, and command me to desire,"
he writes. "My mother endorses them, too. She is
silently brutishly willing me to get married and
breed grandchildren for her. Her will is the will of
Nearly Everybody, and in their will is my death. *My*
will is to live according to my nature, and to find a
place where I can be what I am." For Isherwood,
homosexuality is not only his nature but also his
way of protesting the heterosexual dictatorship. "If
boys didn't exist," he admits, "I should have to in-
vent them."

Indeed, his sexuality is finally revealed as the
basic source of his eventual disaffection from the
leftist political causes that he had endorsed in the
1930s. He made their treatment of the homosexual
the supreme test by which to judge every political
group, challenging each, "All right, we've heard
your liberty speech. Does that include us or doesn't
it?" Although the Soviet Union originally passed
this test by legalizing consensual homosexuality in
1917, Stalin's repressive government joined the
Western democracies in outlawing all homosexual
acts in 1934. At first Christopher, like many other
leftists, attempts to minimize communism's betrayal of its own ideals; but he finally realizes that
"he must dissociate himself from the Communists,
even as a fellow traveler." He resolves never again
to "give way to embarrassment, never deny the
rights of his tribe, never apologize for its existence,
never think of sacrificing himself masochistically
on the altar of that false god of the totalitarians, the
Greatest Good of the Greatest Number—whose
priests are alone empowered to decide what 'good'
is."

The novelistic structure of the book is the saga
of Christopher and Heinz. A working-class boy with
whom Christopher falls in love early in his Berlin

days, Heinz becomes the most important individual in Christopher's life during the 1930s. "Christopher had no hesitation in falling in love with Heinz," Isherwood explains. "It seemed most natural to him that they two should be drawn together. Heinz had found his elder brother; Christopher had found someone emotionally innocent, entirely vulnerable and uncritical, whom he could protect and cherish as his very own."

After Hitler comes to power, the pleasant bohemian life in Berlin turns ugly, and Christopher and Heinz embark in search of refuge. Moving from one European city to another, the two restlessly seek a haven where Heinz can live outside Germany. Despite the expenditure of a thousand pounds—lent by Christopher's mother, Kathleen, who, as Peter Stansky observes, "emerges much more attractively than perhaps the author intends"[7]—and possibly as the result of a betrayal by Gerald Hamilton, the model for Mr. Norris, Heinz is unable to obtain a passport. He is arrested in 1937 and sentenced to prison and then to service in the German army. Rather miraculously, Heinz survives both the imprisonment and the war, and he and Christopher meet again afterwards.

But the forced induction of Heinz into the German army on the eve of the Second World War is what finally convinces Christopher of his pacifism. Aboard the ship taking him and Auden to the United States early in 1939, Christopher asks himself, "Suppose . . . I have a Nazi Army at my mercy. I can blow it up by pressing a button. The men in that Army are notorious for torturing and murdering civilians—all except one of them, Heinz. Will I press the button? No—wait: Suppose I know that Heinz himself, out of cowardice or moral infection, has become as bad as they are and takes part in all their crimes? Will I press that button, even so?"

The answer, "given without the slightest hesitation, was: Of course not." As Gore Vidal remarks of this passage, "That is the voice of humanism in a bad time."[8]

Christopher and His Kind is enriched by its treasure of literary anecdotes and by its wealth of character portraits. Such important literary figures of the 1930s as Auden, Spender, Forster, John Lehmann, Cyril Connolly, Edward Upward, Virginia Woolf, André Gide, and Somerset Maugham are featured. In addition, there is a wonderful account of the German gay liberation pioneer Magnus Hirschfeld, founder of Berlin's Institute for Sexual Science.

The portraits of Forster and Auden are especially moving. Honoring Forster as "the only living writer whom he would have described as his master," Isherwood observes that behind his mentor's "charming, unalarming exterior, was the moralist; and those baby eyes looked very deep into you." Auden, on the other hand, is portrayed as a friend rather than as the leader of the "Auden Generation." When the poet embarks in early 1937 for a stint as an ambulance driver in the Spanish Civil War, his parting from Christopher "made them aware how absolutely each relied on the other's continuing to exist." Explaining that their friendship was rooted in schoolboy memories, Isherwood acknowledges that he and Auden "had been going to bed together, unromantically but with much pleasure, for the past ten years. . . . They couldn't think of themselves as lovers, yet sex had given friendship an extra dimension."

Christopher and His Kind is especially valuable for the correctives it offers to the author's fictionalized accounts of his life during the 1930s. Throughout, Isherwood contrasts the actual events of his experience with the artistic renderings of them, and the real-life models of such characters as Sally Bowles, Mr. Norris, Bernhard and Natalia Landauer, Otto, Friedrich Bergmann, and Ambrose with their depictions in the novels. These contrasts prove illuminating and help define Isherwood's aesthetic as—in Alan Wilde's words—"a distrust of invention, along with a guilty pleasure in its practice; a disarmingly ingenuous equation of fiction and lying; and a fundamental allegiance, even in the area of fiction, to fact."[9] Unfortunately, however, this aesthetic leads Isherwood in *Christopher and His Kind* to devalue unjustly some of his most brilliant fictional techniques.

The book ends with the event in Isherwood's life that proved even more decisive than his visit to Berlin: his emigration to the United States with Auden. In his remarkable final paragraph, Isherwood looks back on the two young men as they are about to begin new lives in America and answers one final question: "Yes, my dears, each of you will find the person you came here to look for—the ideal companion to whom you can reveal yourself totally and yet be loved for what you are, not what you pretend to be." For Auden that ideal companion is Chester Kallman, whom he will meet within three months and with whom he will spend most of the rest of his life. Christopher, on the other hand, will have to wait much longer for his life's companion: "He is already living in the city where you will settle. He will be near you for many years without your meeting. But it would be no good if you did meet now. At present, he is only four years old." The reference is to Don Bachardy, to whom the book is dedicated some twenty-three years after their eventual meeting in 1953.

Christopher and His Kind is a brilliant autobiography that objectively—but not dispassionately—revises the received history of a fascinating decade.

A vigorous defense of individual liberty, it eloquently bears witness to the major significance of homosexuality in Isherwood's life and art. The militancy of Isherwood's commitment to gay liberation invigorates and humanizes the book. Beautifully written and complexly structured with the artistic integrity of a novel, *Christopher and His Kind* is informed with the wisdom of a serene maturity and the exuberance of a still youthful spirit.

My Guru and His Disciple

Published in 1980, *My Guru and His Disciple* begins where *Christopher and His Kind* concludes, with the arrival of Auden and Isherwood in New York near the end of January 1939. A "one-sided, highly subjective story" of Isherwood's relationship with his guru, Swami Prabhavananda, who was for a long time the head of the Vedanta Society of Southern California, *My Guru and His Disciple* is a spiritual autobiography that recounts its author's sometimes painful, frequently humorous, and finally liberating search for God. At the heart of the book is the belief that "the tie between the guru and his initiated disciple cannot be broken, either in this world or on any future plane of existence, until the disciple recognizes the *Atman* within himself and is thus set free."

My Guru and His Disciple concludes with a 1979 postscript written three years after the death of Prabhavananda, but the bulk of the story involves Isherwood's spiritual crises of the early 1940s. The author's interest in Vedanta grew from his attempts to discover positive values to replace his lost political faith; "it was the lack of values which was making me feel so insecure," he remarks of his demoralization soon after arriving in New York. At the invitation of Gerald Heard—the religious philoso-

pher and a fellow expatriate Briton, the model for
Augustus Parr in *Down There on a Visit* and one of
the world's "few great magic mythmakers and re-
vealers of life's wonder"—Isherwood departed for
Los Angeles on May 6, 1939, in search of "a new
self here, an American me." After preparing his visi-
tor to receive Prabhavananda's teaching, Heard introduced him to the swami. "It was Gerald's acceptance of Prabhavananda," Isherwood reveals,
"which made me willing to accept him, at any rate
until I was able to form an opinion of my own."

Isherwood's decision to visit California neces-
sitated his parting with Auden: "I had felt sad to be
leaving Wystan behind but nothing would have in-
duced him to come; he was busy and happy in New
York." Their relationship was altered not because
their love had diminished but because they no
longer had to rely on each other. "When we had
sailed from England that January," Isherwood reflects, "our futures seemed interlocked for good or
ill; we were a mated, isolated couple. America was
to have been our joint adventure. But it was America, which, literally, came between us." Years later,
after Isherwood has converted to Vedantism and
Auden has found renewed faith in Anglicanism, the
two are briefly reunited for long, intimate talks.
During one of these, Auden expresses regret over
Isherwood's conversion—"All this heathen mumbo
jumbo—I'm sorry, my dear, but it just won't *do*."
But "in the abrupt, dismissive tone which he used
when making an unwilling admission," Auden
adds: "Your Swami's quite obviously a saint, of
course."

Isherwood's Swami emerges in the book as a
fascinating figure, one who combines deep and un-
affected spirituality with human charm and vanity.
Prabhavananda's minor flaws—his occasional pettiness, nationalistic pride, competitiveness, and ap-

preciation of worldly comforts—serve not only to
humanize him but also to prompt the book's insistence on a crucial distinction between his dual roles
in Isherwood's life: as an engaging individual who
was born Abanindra Nath Ghosh in Bengal in 1894,
and as "The Guru," a spiritual teacher who exists
only to help his disciples, a receptacle of "'this
thing,' the Eternal." The roles prove to be complementary, for Isherwood's personal affection for
Prabhavananda was a necessary component in his
acceptance of the swami's belief. Near the end of
the book, Isherwood reveals the growth of his own
spiritual perception by noting that "Abanindra,
with his weaknesses *and* his virtues, is fading away,
while 'this thing,' which has always been present
within him, is becoming more and more evident."

Inasmuch as the search for a father is a major
theme in *Prater Violet*, Isherwood's first novel written in America, it is not surprising that in this autobiographical account of his American years the
dominant metaphor for the guru-disciple bond is
that of the father-son relationship. Isherwood movingly portrays Prabhavananda as his symbolic father. Writing of the period after he had disappointed his guru by abandoning a monastic
vocation, Isherwood remarks, "My visits to Swami
were like those of a Prodigal Son who returns home
again and again, without the least intention of stay-
ing, and is always uncritically welcomed by a Father who scolds every other member of the family
for the smallest backsliding." At another point,
Prabhavananda describes Isherwood as "my disciple and my child"; and when the writer qualifies
himself as "a very silly child," the Swami adds: "Oh
no, Chris, you are the most intelligent of my children."

My Guru and His Disciple is also deeply revealing of Isherwood's other personal relationships,

particularly his emotional involvements with several young men: Vernon, who accompanied him to Los Angeles; Denny Fouts, the model for Paul in *Down There on a Visit*; Alfred, a strikingly beautiful youth whom he sometimes treated as "one of the seven deadly sins, which might be overcome by overindulgence"; and Bill Caskey, with whom he lived for several years and whose photographs illustrate *The Condor and the Cows*.

Appropriately, one evidence of Isherwood's growing maturity is that the lasting union he finally achieves with Don Bachardy is one in which he at least initially assumes a paternal role. When the two of them met in 1953, Bachardy was only eighteen years old. "The thirty-year difference in our ages shocked some of those who knew us," Isherwood acknowledges. "I myself didn't feel guilty about this, but I did feel awed by the emotional intensity of our relationship, right from its beginning; the strange sense of a fated, mutual discovery. I knew that, this time, I had really committed myself. Don might leave me, but I couldn't possibly leave him, unless he ceased to need me. The sense of responsibility which was almost fatherly made me anxious but full of joy." Eventually, Bachardy also embraces Vedantism, and he and Isherwood become householder members of the Vedanta Society.

My Guru and His Disciple is helpful in illuminating the religious points of view that inform Isherwood's later novels. The novels themselves are not discussed in detail, but the spiritual autobiography neatly encapsulates in personal terms the values they incorporate. Central to understanding the novels, for instance, is an appreciation of some key differences between Vedanta and Christianity, differences that help explain Isherwood's spiritual conversion after a long history of rebellion against conventional religiosity. Foremost among these dif-

ferences are the contrasting attitudes toward homosexuality. Prabhavananda passes Isherwood's first
test when he reveals not the least shadow of distaste
for homosexual relationships: "From that moment
on, I began to understand that the Swami did not
think in terms of sin, as most Christians do. Certainly, he regarded my lust for Vernon as an obstacle
to my spiritual progress—but no more and no less of
an obstacle than lust for a woman, even for a law-
fully wedded wife, would have been."

Another difference between Christianity and
Vedanta is that the language of the latter was new to
Isherwood and did not contain for him those associations of cant and hypocrisy that the language of
conventional Christianity did. Although in the early
stages of their relationship, Isherwood frequently
complained that "the Swami is too Indian for me,"
he finally admits that the very foreignness of Vedanta was helpful to him: "Because of my other,
anti-Christian set of prejudices, I was repelled by
the English religious words I had been taught in
childhood and was grateful to Vedanta for speaking
Sanskrit. I needed a brand-new vocabulary and
here it was, with a set of philosophical terms which
were exact in meaning, unemotive, untainted by
disgusting old associations with clergymen's ser-
mons, schoolmasters' pep talks, politicians' patriotic
speeches." And, finally, unlike Christianity, Vedanta is nondogmatic: it recognizes the validity of
other paths to spiritual enlightenment, a stance perfectly suited to Isherwood's own temperament.

Indeed, the absence of dogmatism is a key fea-
ture of this luminous autobiography. Affirming that
he is unable to speak "with the absolute authority of
a knower," Isherwood offers *My Guru and His Disciple* to his fellow travelers on the journey through
life "in the hope that it may somehow to some
readers, reveal glimpses of inner truth which re-

main hidden from its author." Beautifully written in a supple prose that combines wit and high seriousness, *My Guru and His Disciple* is a compelling account of the spiritual quest. Its glimpses of inner truth illuminate the life and work of one of America's most remarkable writers.

Isherwood's autobiographies succeed largely because of his novelistic gift of portraying himself as "a central character to whom all other characters and all events are directly related, and by whose mind all experiences are subjectively judged."[10] They are enriched by the continuity of consciousness that enables him both to reinterpret his past in terms of the present and to view his earlier selves as inchoate versions of his current state. No other contemporary writer has been so productively preoccupied with the interpretation of the enormous journey through life, a journey that Isherwood has not yet completed and that promises to yield still more glimpses of inner truth.

10

~~~~~~

Afterword

Like Proust, Christopher Isherwood discovered the source of his art in the mirror. But having lived, as Paul Piazza observes, "in the center, or on the border, of the dangers and difficulties, the terrible Tests of our time,"[1] Isherwood found in his mirror the personal reflection of universal predicaments. He may be the most narrowly self-absorbed of all contemporary novelists; yet his novels and autobiographies are never self-indulgent. They confront the most vital issues of contemporary life. Again and again, they wrestle with questions of alienation and isolation, of involvement and commitment, of sexuality and spirituality: issues that haunt the twentieth-century psyche.

Among our most distinguished living writers, Isherwood is notoriously uneven. All of his books are genuinely worth reading, but their quality varies. *The Last of Mr. Norris* is less ambitious than *Goodbye to Berlin; The Memorial* is a far more mature achievement than *All the Conspirators; The World in the Evening* suffers in comparison with *Down There on a Visit; A Single Man* is rivaled only by *Goodbye to Berlin*. But despite the temptations to compare the books to each other and to separate the periods of his career—the English Isherwood as opposed to the Berlin Isherwood as opposed to the

American or Vedantic Isherwood—there is a real
sense in which all his work is of a single thread. He
described Katherine Mansfield as "among the most
personal and subjective of modern writers; and, in
her case, fiction and autobiography form a single,
indivisible opus."[2] The same can be said of him and
his work.

The achievement of Isherwood's "single, indivisible opus" earns him a special place in Anglo-
American literary history. Its lessons are the sus-
taining values of "humanism in a bad time." The
product of scrupulous self-examination, penetrating
insight, and technical virtuosity, Isherwood's work
illustrates the power of irony and the triumph of
honesty. In a voice uniquely his own, tinged with
humor and compassion, Isherwood illuminates the
human conflicts of our time, translating them into
the universal form of art. Auden's injunction in a
1937 poem written for his friend, whom he charac-
terizes as a brilliant young novelist—observant,
witty, profound, and willful—remains pertinent
some forty-three years later: *"Use your will. We
need it."*[3]

Notes

1. THAT ENORMOUS JOURNEY: A BIOGRAPHICAL SKETCH

1. For complete biographical information, see Jonathan Fryer, *Isherwood: A Biography of Christopher Isherwood* (London: New English Library, 1977); and Brian Finney, *Christopher Isherwood: A Critical Biography* (New York: Oxford University Press, 1979). See also Isherwood's autobiographical works and the discussions of them in chapter 9 of the present book.
2. Isherwood, "What Vedanta Means to Me," in *What Vedanta Means to Me: A Symposium*, ed. John Yale (Garden City, N.Y.: Doubleday, 1960), p. 54.
3. Ibid., p. 57.
4. Carolyn G. Heilbrun, *Christopher Isherwood*, Columbia Essays on Modern Writers 53 (New York: Columbia University Press, 1970), pp. 45-46.
5. Gore Vidal, "Art, Sex and Isherwood," *New York Review of Books* 23 (December 9, 1976):18.

2. ELEGIES FOR A DYING CITY: THE BERLIN STORIES

1. Isherwood, "About This Book," *The Berlin Stories* (New York: New Directions, 1954), p. v.
2. Paul Piazza, *Christopher Isherwood: Myth and*

Anti-Myth (New York: Columbia University Press, 1978), pp. 88-89.

3. The best studies of Isherwood's prose style are two discussions by Alan Wilde—*Christopher Isherwood*, Twayne's United States Authors Series 173 (New York: Twayne, 1971), pp. 14-18, and "Language and Surface: Isherwood and the Thirties," *Contemporary Literature* 16 (1975):478-91.
4. Isherwood, "About This Book," p. vi.
5. For an excellent discussion of the significance of Norris's link with *fin de siècle* romanticism, see Peter Thomas, "'Camp' and Politics in Isherwood's Berlin Fiction," *Journal of Modern Literature* 5 (1976):117–30.
6. See Carl G. Jung et al., *Man and His Symbols* (Garden City, N.Y.: Doubleday, 1964), pp. 167-76.
7. Isherwood, Author's Note for *Goodbye to Berlin*, (London: Hogarth, 1939), p. 287.
8. Stanley Poss, "A Conversation on Tape," *London Magazine*, NS 1 (June 1961):43.
9. Sigmund Freud, *Beyond the Pleasure Principle*, in *The Complete Psychological Works of Sigmund Freud*, vol. 18, trans. James Strachey et al. (London: Hogarth, 1955), p. 32.
10. Wilde, *Christopher Isherwood*, p. 73.
11. The real-life model for Sally Bowles was Jean Ross, an English girl who lived in Berlin during Isherwood's residence there. But Isherwood may also have been influenced by his conception of a period in the life of Katherine Mansfield, one of his early literary idols. See his discussion of Mansfield in *Exhumations*, pp. 64-72.
12. Samuel Hynes, *The Auden Generation: Literature and Politics in England in the 1930s* (London: Bodley Head, 1976), p. 358.
13. Otto Friedrich, *Before the Deluge: A Portrait of Berlin in the 1920's* (New York: Harper & Row, 1972), p. 303.
14. Heilbrun, *Christopher Isherwood*, p. 4.

3.   EVIL MOTHERS AND TRULY WEAK MEN:
All the Conspirators, The Memorial,
COLLABORATIONS WITH AUDEN

1. Cyril Connolly, Introduction to *All the Conspirators*, (London: Traveller's Library, Jonathan Cape, 1939), p. 7.
2. Isherwood, Foreword to *All the Conspirators* (New York: New Directions, 1958), p. 9.
3. Brian Finney, *Christopher Isherwood: A Critical Biography*, p. 75.
4. Frank Kermode, *Puzzles and Epiphanies: Essays and Reviews 1958–1961* (London: Routledge & Kegan Paul, 1962), p. 126.
5. On this point, see Walter Allen, *The Modern Novel in Britain and the United States* (New York: Dutton, 1964), pp. 236-37.
6. Paul Piazza, *Christopher Isherwood: Myth and Anti-Myth*, p. 38.
7. Stephen Spender, "The Poetic Dramas of W. H. Auden and Christopher Isherwood," *New Writing*, NS 1 (London: Hogarth, 1938), pp. 102-103.
8. For an account of the collaboration on the plays and of each author's individual contribution to them, see Edward Mendelson, "The Auden-Isherwood Collaboration," *Twentieth Century Literature* 22 (1976):276–85. For an account of the Group Theatre, see Julian Symons, *The Thirties: A Dream Revolved* (London: Faber, 1960; reprinted 1975), pp. 76-84.
9. W. H. Auden, "I Want the Theatre to Be . . .," theater program, Group Theatre Season 1935; reprinted in Hynes, *The Auden Generation*, p. 399.
10. Isherwood, review of A. W. Lawrence, ed., *T. E. Lawrence by His Friends*, in *The Listener*, 17 (1937): 1170; reprinted in *Exhumations*, p. 24.
11. E. M. Forster, *Howards End* (London: Edward Arnold, 1910; reprinted New York: Vintage, 1960), p. 195.

4. THE PAIN OF HUNGER BENEATH EVERYTHING: *Prater Violet*

1. For a politically oriented discussion of this issue, see James T. Farrell, *Literature and Morality* (New York: Vanguard, 1947), pp. 125-32.

2. Isherwood, "Religion without Prayers," *Vedanta and the West*, 9 (1946):106-11; reprinted in *Vedanta for Modern Man*, ed. Christopher Isherwood (New York: Harper, 1951; reprinted New York: New American Library, 1972), pp. 44-49; the quotation is from p. 48 of the later reprint. The entire essay is important, for it contrasts Vedantism with humanistic materialism.

3. Isherwood, "The Gita and War," *Vedanta and the West*, 7 (1944):153-60; reprinted in *Vedanta for the Western World*, ed. Christopher Isherwood (Hollywood: Vedanta Press, 1946), pp. 358–65, and in *Exhumations*, pp. 103-11; the quotation is from *Exhumations*, p. 110.

4. Paul Piazza, *Christopher Isherwood: Myth and Anti-Myth*, pp. 65-72, admirably demonstates the importance of the Bhagavad Gita to *Prater Violet*. In the passage under discussion, however, there are even closer parallels with the *Divine Comedy*; see especially Canto 27 of the *Purgatorio*. For a Vedantic View of Dante, see Guido Ferrando, "The Spiritual Message of Dante," in *Vedanta for the Western World*, pp. 389-95.

5. Isherwood, "The Problem of the Religious Novel," *Vedanta and the West*, 9 (1946):61-64; reprinted in *Vedanta for Modern Man*, pp. 273-77, and in *Exhumations*, pp. 116-20; the quotations are from *Exhumations*, pp. 119 and 118 respectively.

6. Dante, *Purgatorio*, Canto 27, lines 115-17; trans. Lawrence Binyon, in *La divina commedia di Dante Alighieri*, ed. C. H. Grandgent (Boston: D. C. Heath, 1933).

7. Diana Trilling, "Fiction in Review," *The Nation*, 17 November 1945, p. 530.
8. Brian Finney, *Christopher Isherwood: A Critical Biography*, p. 190.
9. Isherwood, *An Approach to Vedanta*, (Hollywood: Vedanta Press, 1963), p. 19.
10. Alan Wilde, *Christopher Isherwood*, p. 100.

5. THEY THAT LOVE BEYOND THE WORLD: *The World in the Evening*

1. Isherwood, letter to Edward Upward, 31 August 1954; quoted in Jonathan Fryer, *Isherwood: A Biography*, p. 248.
2. For an elaboration on the significance of Camp, see Susan Sontag, "Notes on Camp," *Partisan Review* 31 (1964):515-30.
3. John Donne, "The Progresse of the Soule," in *The Complete Poetry and Selected Prose of John Donne*, ed. Charles M. Coffin (New York: Modern Library, 1952), p. 110.
4. *The Riverside Shakespeare*, ed. G. Blakemore Evans et al. (Boston: Houghton Mifflin, 1974), p. 1766.
5. Isherwood, *An Approach to Vedanta*, p. 46.

6. A CONTINUITY OF CONSCIOUSNESS: *Down There on a Visit*

1. Aldous Huxley, Introduction to *The Song of God: Bhagavad-Gita*, trans. Swami Prabhavananda and Christopher Isherwood (New York: New American Library, 1954), p. 13.
2. Alan Wilde, *Christopher Isherwood*, pp. 123-24, briefly discusses this tradition and includes in it such writers as Baudelaire, Dostoevski, Huysmans, Genet, and T. S. Eliot. To this list might be added

Oscar Wilde, particularly since Paul is specifically *compared to Dorian Gray. J. K. Huysmans' Là Bas* is especially important, as it is the source of Isherwood's title.

3. Isherwood, "A Visit to Anselm Oakes," in *Exhumations*, pp. 241-54; the quotation is from p. 253.
4. The term "apotheosis" is Alan Wilde's; see his *Christopher Isherwood*, p. 123.
5. Brian Finney, *Christopher Isherwood: A Critical Biography*, p. 246.

7. THE WATERS OF THE POOL: *A Single Man*

1. Paul Piazza, *Christopher Isherwood: Myth and Anti-Myth*, p. 150.
2. Jonathan Raban, *The Technique of Modern Fiction* (London: Edward Arnold, 1968), p. 32.
3. Carolyn G. Heilbrun, *Christopher Isherwood*, p. 42.
4. Dennis Altman, *Homosexual Oppression and Liberation* (New York: Avon, 1973), pp. 50-51.
5. Alan Wilde, *Christopher Isherwood*, pp. 128-29.
6. Aldous Huxley, Introduction to *The Song of God, Bhagavad-Gita*, p. 16.
7. Ibid.
8. Wilde, *Christopher Isherwood*, p. 137.
9. Altman, *Homosexual Oppression and Liberation*, p. 39.

8. THE ONLY THING THAT REALLY MATTERS: *A Meeting by the River*

1. Isherwood, letter to Alan White, 21 April 1967; quoted in Brian Finney, *Christopher Isherwood: A Critical Biography*, p. 263.
2. John Gross, "A Question of Upbringing," *New York Review of Books* 8 (May 18, 1967):36.
3. For a discussion of the humor in the novel, see Paul Piazza, *Christopher Isherwood: Myth and Anti-Myth*, pp. 166-67.

9. Glimpses of Inner Truth: Biography And Autobiography

1. Isherwood, Foreword to "The Railway Accident" by Allen Chalmers (Edward Upward) in *New Directions in Prose and Poetry XI*, ed. James Laughlin (New York: New Directions, 1949), p. 84.

2. Isherwood, letter to John Lehmann, 6 November 1948; quoted in Brian Finney, *Christopher Isherwood: A Critical Biography,* p. 201.

3. Stanley Poss, "A Conversation on Tape," p. 52.

4. "Mr. Isherwood Changes Trains," *Times Literary Supplement*, 11 November 1949, p. 727.

5. Finney, *Christopher Isherwood: A Critical Biography*, p. 203.

6. W. H. Auden, "The Diary of a Diary," *New York Review of Books*, 18 (January 27, 1972):19.

7. Peter Stansky, review of *Christopher and His Kind*, in *The New York Times Book Review*, 28 November 1976, p. 34.

8. Gore Vidal, "Art, Sex and Isherwood," p. 18.

9. Alan Wilde, review of *Christopher and His Kind*, in *Journal of Modern Literature* 6 (1977):485.

10. Isherwood, review of Stephen Spender, *World Within World*, in *Tomorrow* 10 (1951):56-59; reprinted in *Exhumations*, pp. 55-64; the quotation is from *Exhumations*, p. 55. The description is of Spender's stance in his autobiography, but applies equally well to Isherwood's strategy in his own autobiographical writings.

10. Afterword

1. Paul Piazza, *Christopher Isherwood: Myth and Anti-Myth*, p. 195.

2. Isherwood, "Katherine Mansfield," in *Exhumations*, p. 65.

3. W. H. Auden, untitled poem, first published in full as an appendix in Brian Finney, *Christopher Isherwood: A Critical Biography*, pp. 287-89.

Bibliography

I. PRINCIPAL WORKS BY CHRISTOPHER ISHERWOOD
(Arranged chronologically)

All the Conspirators. London: Jonathan Cape, 1928.

Translator. *Intimate Journals* by Charles Baudelaire. Introduction by T. S. Eliot. London: Blackmore, 1930. Revised edition. Introduction by W. H. Auden. Hollywood: Marcel Rodd, 1947.

The Memorial: Portrait of a Family. London: Hogarth, 1932.

The Last of Mr. Norris. New York: Morrow, 1935. [British title: *Mr. Norris Changes Trains*. London: Hogarth, 1935.]

With W. H. Auden. *The Dog Beneath the Skin, or Where is Francis? A Play in Three Acts*. London: Faber, 1935.

With W. H. Auden. *The Ascent of F 6, a Tragedy in Two Acts*. London: Faber, 1936.

Sally Bowles. London: Hogarth, 1937.

Lions and Shadows: An Education in the Twenties. London: Hogarth, 1938.

With W. H. Auden. *On the Frontier: A Melodrama in Three Acts*. London: Faber, 1938.

With W. H. Auden. *Journey to a War*. London: Faber, 1939.

Goodbye to Berlin. New York: Random House, 1939.

Translator, with Swami Prabhavananda. *The Song of God: Bhagavad-Gita*. Hollywood: Marcel Rodd, 1944.

Editor. *Vedanta for the Western World*. Hollywood: Marcel Rodd, 1945.

171

Prater Violet. New York: Random House, 1945.

Translator, with Swami Prabhavananda. *Shankara's Crest-Jewel of Discrimination*. Hollywood: Vedanta Press, 1947.

The Condor and the Cows: A South American Travel Diary. New York: Random House, 1949.

Editor. *Vedanta for Modern Man*. New York: Harper, 1951.

Translator, with Swami Prabhavananda. *How to Know God: The Yoga Aphorisms of Patanjali*. New York: Harper, 1953.

The World in the Evening. New York: Random House, 1954.

Editor. *Great English Short Stories*. New York: Dell, 1957.

Down There on a Visit. New York: Simon & Schuster, 1962.

An Approach to Vedanta. Hollywood: Vedanta Press, 1963.

A Single Man. New York: Simon & Schuster, 1964.

Ramakrishna and His Disciples. New York: Simon & Schuster, 1965.

Exhumations: Stories, Articles, Verses. New York: Simon & Schuster, 1966.

A Meeting by the River. New York: Simon & Schuster, 1967.

Kathleen and Frank: The Autobiography of a Family. New York: Simon & Schuster, 1971.

With Don Bachardy. *Frankenstein: The True Story*. New York: Avon, 1973.

Christopher and His Kind, 1929-1939. New York: Farrar, Straus & Giroux, 1976.

My Guru and His Disciple. New York: Farrar, Straus & Giroux, 1980.

II. WORKS ABOUT CHRISTOPHER ISHERWOOD

Bibliographies

Funk, Robert W. *Christopher Isherwood: A Reference Guide*. Boston: G. K. Hall, 1979.

Orphanis, Stathis. "Christopher Isherwood: A Checklist 1968-1975." *Twentieth Century Literature* 22 (1976):354-61.

Westby, Selmer, and Brown, Clayton M. *Christopher Isherwood: A Bibliography 1923-1967*. Los Angeles: California State College at Los Angeles Foundation, 1968.

Selected Biographical and Critical Studies

Allen, Walter. *The Modern Novel in Britain and the United States*. New York: Dutton, 1964. [British title: *Tradition and Dreams: The English and American Novel from the Twenties to Our Time*. London: Phoenix House, 1964.]

Brogan, Hugh. "*Lions and Shadows*." *Twentieth Century Literature* 22 (1976):303-11.

Connolly, Cyril. *Enemies of Promise and Other Essays*. New York: Macmillan, 1938.

———. Introduction to *All the Conspirators*. London: Jonathan Cape, 1939.

Dempsey, David. "Connolly, Orwell, and Others: An English Miscellany." *Antioch Review* 7 (1947):142-50.

Dewsnap, Terence. "Isherwood Couchant." *Critique: Studies in Modern Fiction* 13 (1970):31-47.

Farrell, James T. "When Graustark Is in Celluloid." In *Literature and Morality*. New York: Vanguard, 1947.

Finney, Brian. *Christopher Isherwood: A Critical Biography*. New York: Oxford University Press, 1979.

———. "Christopher Isherwood: A Profile." *The New Review*, August 1975, pp. 17-24.

———. "Laily, Mortmere and All That." *Twentieth Century Literature* 22 (1976):286-302.

Forster, E. M. *Two Cheers for Democracy*. London: Edward Arnold, 1951.

Fryer, Jonathan. *Isherwood: A Biography of Christopher Isherwood*. London: New English Library, 1977.

———. "Sexuality in Isherwood." *Twentieth Century Literature* 22 (1976):343-53.

Gerstenberger, Donna. "Poetry and Politics: The Verse Drama of Auden and Isherwood." *Modern Drama* 5 (1962):123-32.

174   Christopher Isherwood

Heilbrun, Carolyn G. *Christopher Isherwood*. Columbia
    Essays on Modern Writers 53. New York: Columbia,
    1970.
Hoggart, Richard. "The Plays with Christopher Isher-
    wood." In *Auden: An Introductory Essay*. London:
    Chatto & Windus, 1951.
Hynes, Samuel L. *The Auden Generation: Literature and
    Politics in England in the 1930s*. London: Bodley
    Head, 1976.
Kermode, Frank. "The Interpretation of the Times," in
    *Puzzles and Epiphanies: Essays and Reviews 1958-
    1961*. London: Routledge, 1962.
King, Francis. *Christopher Isherwood*. Writers and Their
    Work 240. Harlow, Essex: Longman, 1976.
Lehmann, John. "Adventures in Drama" and "Refitting
    the Novel." In *New Writing in Europe*. Har-
    mondsworth: Penguin, 1942.
————. *In My Own Time: Memoirs of a Literary Life*.
    Boston: Little, Brown, 1969.
————. "Two of the Conspirators." *Twentieth Century
    Literature* 22 (1976):264-75.
Maes-Jelinek, Hena. *Criticism of Society in the English
    Novel Between the Wars*. Paris: Société d'Editions
    "Les Belles Lettres," 1970.
————. "The Knowledge of Man in the Works of Chris-
    topher Isherwood." *Revue des Langues Vivantes* 26
    (1960):341-60.
Mayne, Richard. "The Novel and Mr. Norris." *Cambridge
    Journal* 6 (1953): 561-70.
Mendelson, Edward. "The Auden-Isherwood Collabora-
    tion." *Twentieth Century Literature* 22 (1976):276-
    85.
Nagarajan, S. "Christopher Isherwood and the Vedantic
    Novel: A Study of *A Single Man*." *Ariel: A Review of
    International English Literature* 3 (1972):63-71.
Piazza, Paul. *Christopher Isherwood: Myth and Anti-
    Myth*. New York: Columbia, 1978.
Pritchett, V. S. "Men of the World." In *The Penguin New
    Writing*, no. 30. Edited by John Lehmann. Har-
    mondsworth: Penguin, 1947.

Raban, Jonathan. *The Technique of Modern Fiction*. London: Edward Arnold, 1968.

Rosenfeld, Isaac. "Isherwood's Master Theme." In *An Age of Enormity: Life and Writing in the Forties and Fifties*. Cleveland: World Publishing, 1962.

Spender, Stephen. "The Auden-Isherwood Collaboration." *New Republic*, 23 November 1959, pp. 16-17.

———. "Notebook—XII." *London Magazine*, April-May 1977, pp. 46-51.

———. *World Within World*. New York: Harcourt, Brace, 1951.

Summers, Claude J. "Christopher Isherwood and the Need for Community." *Perspectives on Contemporary Literature* 3 (1977):30-37.

Thomas, David P. "*Goodbye to Berlin*: Refocusing Isherwood's Camera." *Contemporary Literature* 13 (1972):44-52.

Thomas, Peter. "'Camp' and Politics in Isherwood's Berlin Fiction." *Journal of Modern Literature* 5 (1976):117-30.

Tolley, A. Trevor. *The Poetry of the Thirties*. New York: St. Martin's, 1976.

Vidal, Gore. "Art, Sex and Isherwood." *New York Review of Books*, 9 December 1976, pp. 10-18.

Viertel, Berthold. "Christopher Isherwood and Dr. Friedrich Bergmann." *Theatre Arts* 30 (1946):295-98.

Weisgerber, Jean. "Les Romans et Récrits de Christopher Isherwood." *Revue de l'Université de Bruxelles* 10 (1958):360-80.

Whitehead, John. "Christophananda Isherwood at Sixty." *London Magazine*, July 1965, pp. 90-100.

Wilde, Alan. *Christopher Isherwood*. Twayne's United States Authors Series 173. New York: Twayne, 1971.

———. "Irony and Style: The Example of Christopher Isherwood." *Modern Fiction Studies* 16 (1970):475-89.

———. "Language and Surface: Isherwood and the Thirties." *Contemporary Literature* 16 (1975):478-91.

Wilson, Angus. "The New and Old Isherwood." *Encounter*, August 1954, pp. 62-68.

Wilson, Colin. "An Integrity Born of Hope: Notes on Christopher Isherwood." *Twentieth Century Literature* 22 (1976):312-31.

III.   SELECTED INTERVIEWS WITH ISHERWOOD

Aitken, Will. "Up Here on a Visit." *Body Politic* (Toronto), no. 32 (April 1977), 12-14.
Geherin, David J. "An Interview with Christopher Isherwood." *Journal of Narrative Technique* 2 (1972): 143-58.
Halpern, Daniel. "A Conversation with Christopher Isherwood." *Antaeus*, 13-14 (1974): 366-88.
Heilbrun, Carolyn G. "Christopher Isherwood: An Interview." *Twentieth Century Literature* 22 (1976):253-63.
Leyland, Winston, and Austen, Roger. "Christopher Isherwood." In *Gay Sunshine Interviews*, I. Edited by Winston Leyland. San Francisco: Gay Sunshine Press, 1978.
Poss, Stanley. "A Conversation on Tape." *London Magazine*, June 1961, pp. 41-58.
Russo, Tony. "Interview with Christopher Isherwood." *Christopher Street*, March 1977, pp. 6-10.
Scobie, W. I. "Christopher Isherwood." In *Writers at Work: The Paris Review Interviews*. 4th series. Edited by George Plimpton. New York: Viking, 1976.
———. "Christopher Isherwood: A Lively Exchange with One of Our Greatest Living Writers." *The Advocate*, 17 December 1975, pp. 6-8.
Wennerstein, Robert. "Christopher Isherwood." *Transatlantic Review*, Spring-Summer 1972, pp. 5-21.
Wickes, George. "An Interview with Christopher Isherwood." *Shenandoah*, Spring 1965, pp. 22-52.

Index

MODERN LITERATURE MONOGRAPHS

In the same series: (continued from page ii)

VLADIMIR NABOKOV   *Donald E. Morton*
ANAIS NIN   *Bettina L. Knapp*
FLANNERY O'CONNOR   *Dorothy Tuck McFarland*
EUGENE O'NEILL   *Horst Frenz*
JOSÉ ORTEGA Y GASSET   *Franz Niedermayer*
GEORGE ORWELL   *Roberta Kalechofsky*
KATHERINE ANNE PORTER   *John Edward Hardy*
EZRA POUND   *Jeannette Lander*
MARCEL PROUST   *James R. Hewitt*
RAINER MARIA RILKE   *Arnold Bauer*
JEAN-PAUL SARTRE   *Liselotte Richter*
UPTON SINCLAIR   *Jon Yoder*
ISAAC BASHEVIS SINGER   *Irving Malin*
LINCOLN STEFFENS   *Robert Stinson*
KURT VONNEGUT   *James Lundquist*
PETER WEISS   *Otto F. Best*
EDITH WHARTON   *Richard H. Lawson*
THORNTON WILDER   *Hermann Stresau*
THOMAS WOLFE   *Fritz Heinrich Ryssel*
VIRGINIA WOOLF   *Manly Johnson*
RICHARD WRIGHT   *David Bakish*
CARL ZUCKMAYER   *Arnold Bauer*